The Doctor's Law Guide:

ESSENTIALS OF PRACTICE MANAGEMENT

MARC J. LANE, J.D.
of the Chicago Bar

1979 W. B. SAUNDERS COMPANY • PHILADELPHIA • LONDON • TORONTO

W. B. Saunders Company: West Washington Square
Philadelphia, Pa. 19105

1 St. Anne's Road
Eastbourne, East Sussex BN21 3UN, England

1 Goldthorne Avenue
Toronto, Ontario M8Z 5T9, Canada

The Doctor's Law Guide:
Essentials of Practice Management   ISBN   0-7216-5609-9

Last digit is the print number: 9   8   7   6   5   4   3   2   1

For
ROCHELLE
with love.

PREFACE

Today is a new day, a day in which every professional should reassess his role, his function, his mandate, indeed his future. No longer is the typical health care provider a humanistic sole practitioner, freely dispensing personal advice to a close circle of friends and neighbors. Instead, he is a compassionate scientist, responsive to consumer, labor, and industrial demands for high-quality, comprehensive service at a reasonable cost.

He may remain a sole practitioner, but he's surely created an informal network of relationships with other professionals on whom he relies daily. He may have joined a group, compensated on a fee-for-service basis. Whatever the mode of his practice, he has learned that specialization carries with it the need to refer, the need to consult, the need to pool and share health care resources.

Improved communications and transportation have fostered the growth of large, centralized group practices with efficiency-conscious decision-making structures. Inevitably, employers and governments have assumed a greater share of the burden of financing and controlling this largest of industries. Medicare and Medicaid, Health Maintenance Organizations, Professional Standards Review Organizations, and the National Health Planning and Resources Development Acts have all played their part in building a quality prepaid health care system. If government and business soon give birth to comprehensive national health insurance, never again may a medical catastrophe reduce a middle-income family to poverty.

These trends are socioeconomically significant; they are reshaping political ideology and overcoming social prejudice. Soon they should responsibly allow the delivery of health care services to all Americans. As an individual provider, you obviously perceive such progress as good. But, at the same time, you should affirmatively react to its consequences for your practice. Consumerism, regulation, and fee constraints dictate that you view what you do as a business—not in any deprecating commercial sense, but as a fiscally controlled professional enterprise geared to maximum high-quality productivity. Adopting this new perspective bears no shame: you and your like-thinking peers will be survivors in the econimic world around the corner. And your patients and communities will become the principal beneficiaries of your good vision.

The Doctor's Law Guide looks at your practice the way you should. Pursuing opportunities, side-stepping pitfalls, it is aimed at providing you with instant answers to legal questions you are apt to have as you conduct your professional practice. What's more, it puts the answers in a definitional context, so that you don't have to wade through pages of prose to find a particular point.

In the early chapters, we cover questions about the structure of your practice, and then we move on to operational areas. Just turn to the chapter you are interested in and start reading. You'll find a short narrative describing the status of the law today, and, in outline form, a more detailed development of the subject. The goal is simplicity, readability, and making common sense out of jargon and business sense out of professional platitudes.

We hope that you will use this book daily. Review it before you call your lawyer and you'll save his time and yours. It will answer routine questions for you immediately, assist you with long-range planning, and prepare you for what's to come.

One final comment: *The Doctor's Law Guide* is not to be taken as gospel. Its approach is general, and what may apply to a California practitioner of six months may not be true for the half-century practitioner in New York. In addition, we are dealing with a subject that is forever changing, forever complicating itself, forever improving.

Now that our philosophy and disclaimers have been said, let's plunge in.

MARC J. LANE, J. D.

CONTENTS

CHAPTER 1

PARTNERSHIPS:
Friction-Free Togetherness

§1.01

WHY SACRIFICE THE INDEPENDENCE?

Many health professionals have found it wise to join together in groups to render their services. Very often, a group practice can be administered more productively and more economically than sole proprietorships can. Assured coverage and ready consultation may be reasons enough.

Yet the pooling of expenses and the sharing of office space alone need not mean that colleagues are now partners. The formation of a legal partnership requires the creation of a new formal relationship, one controlled by common law, by statute, by mutual understanding, and, ideally, by written contract.

§1.02

HOW YOUR CONTRACT WILL LOOK

Reducing rights and obligations to a document is always a good idea. Potential issues of dispute can be resolved in advance; major negotiable issues can be decided during organizational discussions, when you still have bargaining power. You will spot the following items in any well-conceived partnership agreement:

1. *The partnership's name.* The selection of the partnership name may be limited by state law and the ethics of your profession. If you intend to include a partner's surname, for instance, bear in mind that some states will require a name change after his or her death. Beyond these rules, avoid any name that is similar to that of an existing partnership. Once you have decided on your partnership name, in most states you will be required to register it at a governmental office, so interested third parties can learn the identity of the principals.

2. *The partnership activity.* Of course, your agreement must require all the partners to comply with relevant licensing laws. However, you may also want to restrict the specialties in which your partnership will be working. That way, all concerned will have a clear appreciation for the practice's goals.

3. *Duration.* Your agreement can be indefinite as to the term of your partnership, or a specific termination date can be set. If your eventually decide to continue your relationship beyond the time your agreement dictates, be safe: renew your contract or, better still, enter into a new one.

Whatever your agreement provides, any partner can resign from the practice whenever he or she chooses and dissolve the partnership. No one can be forced to perform a service against his or her will; our constitution prohibits involuntary servitude. Nevertheless, your contract can exert muscle; if your partner resigns in violation of your agreement, you can sue for damages.

Damages in such cases are often speculative and difficult to value in dollars and cents. That is why your agreement can prescribe "liquidated damages"—a reasonable prediction of the extent to which one partner would cause the other partners to suffer by resigning prematurely.

4. *Contributions.* Before the partnership can become operative, each of you must contribute your share of the cash, property, and services which will be known as "the partnership capital." You will then have a stake in whatever property the partnership funds are used to buy.

Your contribution will not be a taxable event, since you will be exchanging your property for an interest in the partnership, and these are assets of equal value. Suppose you paid $5,000 for a parcel of land in 1975, and since then it has doubled in value. Now you want to contribute it to the partnership as the site of its future office building. Your partnership will credit you with the full value you contribute, $10,000. In addition, you will not have to pay any personal income tax on the $5,000 growth in your investment. Years from now, should the partnership sell the land you are contributing, all the partners will be taxed on any proceeds they net over and above the $5,000 you originally paid.

You can change this result by prior agreement. With regard to any or all contributed property, the partnership's ultimate tax gain or loss can be allocated among the partners, taking into account any difference between the property's basis and its value at the time it is contributed.

[See §5.11] 5. *Sales, loans, and leases.* It may be easier and fairer for you to sell property to the partnership and realize a taxable gain or loss immediately. Another alternative is to loan property and receive interest or rent on it from the partnership. This way you will be insulating your asset from the claims of partnership creditors, since it will never become partnership capital. If the rent you receive approximates deductible depreciation, they will tend to offset each other, and the partnership can deduct the rent.

6. *Your income as a partner.* A partner is not usually paid a salary for the services he or she performs, except for efforts to terminate the partnership's affairs at its conclusion. Of course, you and your partners can agree otherwise, and any salary which the partnership does pay is a tax-deductible expense.

More often, though, partnership agreements restrict each participant's income to his or her share of the profits. Unequal financial contributions often call for inequality in the distribution of profits. Moreover, different kinds of income may be distributed in different ratios, so you may receive 50 per cent of the partnership's operating income, but only 30 per cent of its capital gains. Another solution would allow the establishment of equal capital accounts, with additional contributions by one or more partners characterized as loans.

Your partnership will not be a taxpayer, but merely an accounting unit. Its only function, so far as the IRS is concerned, will be to report information annually: how much income was earned, and what deductible expenses were incurred? You, and not the practice as such, will then be obliged to pay a tax on your proportionate share of profits—less any partnership losses that you have agreed will be attributable to you—whether or not the difference is actually paid out to you.

[See Chapter 5] 7. *The withdrawal of capital.* You may, in fact, want to limit the partners' ability to withdraw monies from the practice. (Remember that big expenditure or investment you and your colleagues are contemplating?) If you do that, each of you should reserve the right to withdraw enough to pay your personal income tax.

8. *The partnership books.* All business records ought to be kept at your principal office, and all the partners ought to have ready access to them. After all, it is your practice. You have both a right and a duty to scrutinize its operation.

9. Management. All partners are equally eligible to conduct the practice as they see fit. So spell out the obligations each partner is to owe to the others. Come to a clear written understanding of each partner's authority to bind the partnership, and impose a "disclosure" duty on all the partners, requiring each to report any information he or she learns which might affect the partnership. This duty might prove crucial: all kinds of knowledge are imputed from one partner to another in a court of law. Courts uniformly conclude that partners should know:

   (a) The terms of their partnership agreement.
   (b) How similar practices operate—"custom and usage."
   (c) The course of their practice's history.

As a health professional, your ethical and legal obligations to your patients and your community demand that you remain aware of what goes on in your partnership. Your partnership, it should be emphasized, may be compelled to indemnify any partner who incurs personal liability during the course of the partnership business—your professional practice. For your own protection, then, remain informed and retain control.

Once you form a partnership, your partnership agreement becomes the foundation of your practice. It sets out your rights and liabilities and, to some degree, can even control which laws apply and which ones need not. To the extent your agreement fails to assign responsibilities, however, local law steps in and makes its own rules.

§1.03

THE UNIFORM PARTNERSHIP ACT

Most states have adopted the Uniform Partnership Act, which was objectively designed to describe what most people *intended* a partnership relationship to be. The Act codifies the common law concept that partners are equal co-owners for the purpose of doing business or, in your case, rendering personal services for monetary gain. As such, every partner is the absolute agent of every other and every partner is the principal of every other, so far as the partnership business is concerned. While the legal consequences of these assumptions are not altogether controllable, some of these generalizations— descriptive of common law partnerships—can be modified to suit you:

- Decision-making is communal; any liability is both individual and collective.
- Taking on a partner clothes him or her with authority beyond that which you may expressly grant, beyond that which you may consciously intend. Additional authority is always implied and incidental: "the power follows the function." Moreover, courts can find authority to avoid harming innocent third parties or to prevent principals from gaining unfair advantages.
- Equality is equity. All partners are entitled to an equal share of partnership profits as their sole compensation.
- The partnership may be liable for the negligence of any partner during the course of partnership business.
- The partnership may also be liable for the negligence of any partner during any act authorized by the partnership. Remember, authority need not be express: if one

[See §8.15]

partner knows of another's plans and remains silent, this silence may be construed as consent.

- As an agent, any partner may withdraw from the partnership at will. Granted, this partner may be liable in money damages to the other partners—the principals—but he or she cannot be compelled to give notice.
- After the partnership has been *dissolved*—that is, after the partners have ceased to render services as a group—all of them have a right to bring the partnership affairs to a close.

§1.04

WHY AN AGREEMENT?

Unless you enter into a comprehensive contract, the law must guess how you would want your partnership to operate, and guesses, it ought to be clear, are sometimes wrong. Take advantage of the consensual nature of a partnership: it begs for prenegotiation and preplanning. Your personal tax situation; your relationship with your prospective partners; the contributions you are willing to make in time, money, services, and property—all these will be important to your lawyer when he drafts a durable contract. If he does a good job, you and your partners will have agreed on where you are today, where you want to be as you approach retirement age, and even how you're going to get there.

§1.05

YOUR PARTNERSHIP AGREEMENT AS AN ESTATE PLANNING TOOL

Your contract will be the plan of action for your team. It will tell you what you are to do, how you are to do it, and how you will be paid for the results. Your agreement can and should serve an even longer-range end—estate planning. As part of your partnership contract or independent of it, it is a good idea to execute a Buy-Sell Agreement. This will assure the continued existence of the practice, even after a partner's death, and guarantees the widow or widower that the partnership interest will be fairly purchased by the surviving partners. There are several steps to follow:

1. Bind the partners [and their spouses too, especially in community property states] to buy the interest of any partner who dies.
2. Obligate each partner's estate to sell his or her interest.
3. Fix the price of the interest and the terms of the sale. Your attorney will guide you through the delicate process of valuation, and show you how payments made by the partnership might be tax-deductible by the practice, or tax-excludable by the decedent's beneficiaries.

[See §12.02]
4. Work out the life insurance requirements and make them contractually binding. Two funding methods are popular:
    (a) The *cross-purchase approach* has each partner buy a policy on the lives of all the others. When one partner dies, the insurance proceeds are paid to the survivors, who use them to purchase the decedent's interest. The policies held by the decedent on the lives of the survivors can then be surrendered.
    (b) The *entity approach*, many times a simpler solution, has each partner contribute a predetermined share of the necessary premiums to the partnership, which then buys policies on the lives of all the partners.

5. You may want to appoint an independent trustee to maintain the various life insurance policies and to administer the agreement as a whole. This individual will be particularly useful if there are several partners or if valuation problems might exist.
6. Release the estate from partnership obligations incurred after the decedent's interest has been sold.

Buy-Sell Agreements are riddled with tax subtleties. Note these three in your tax and estate planning:

- While life insurance premiums are not tax-deductible, policy proceeds, whether they are paid to the surviving partners or to the partnership, are not taxable.
- Your agreement can require the survivors to pay a decedent's heirs or estate a fixed amount or a share of profits periodically, beyond the cost of the partnership interest. Such payments are fully deductible from the survivors' taxable income.
- A decedent's interest in the partnership is valued as of the day he or she dies. This value, excluding any undistributed income the decedent earned, is the tax basis of the asset when it reaches the hands of the heirs, so they are not taxed on any payment they receive for the partnership interest in fixed assets and goodwill.

§1.06

CONCLUSIONS

At best, your partnership can be a long-lasting, easy-to-regulate network of relationships, governed largely by your demands and aspirations. At worst, it can be a chaotic trap, a maze of personal liabilities and adverse tax consequences. The difference is a competently drawn agreement, one which equitably resolves the host of organizational questions you will encounter daily as you care for your patients in the group context.

CHAPTER **2**

KEOGH PLANS AND
IRAS:
Much Ado About
Something

§2.01

THE KEOGH TREND

In increasing numbers, sole practitioners and partners alike are planning for retirement by participating in tax-favored Keogh plans. The Self-Employed Individuals Tax Retirement Act—you probably know it as the Keogh Act—lets self-employed health professionals accumulate retirement dollars in a tax-sheltered way.

§2.02

HOW KEOGH WORKS

The Keogh rules are highly technical and strictly enforced. These are the most important:

1. *Don't forget your employees.* Keogh lets you contribute a part of your income to a fund created to help support you after retirement. Remember, however, that the Act seeks to benefit your staff as well. Any full-time employee who has been with you for three years or more must be included in your plan. To qualify as full-time, an employee must work more than twenty hours weekly and more than five months annually. As you'll see, you may want to include other employees too, and you can. The guidelines here represent minimum standards; you can always be more liberal when you set out your plan's eligibility criteria. Many health professionals give their employees a retirement program instead of a raise. Keogh probably will not cost you more than the salary increases they expect, and retirement benefits are tax-sheltered.

2. *Provide for "immediate vesting."* While you can regulate the time and manner in which Keogh benefits will be distributed, the cash contributions you make to the plan on behalf of your employees, plus any earnings on those contributions, are irrevocably theirs once contributed. That is generally the case even if they quit the next week, or even if they are fired. This is true because the government

reasons that you will never lose the contributions you will make on your own behalf, so why should your employees be subject to less favorable treatment?

3. *Keep your percentages fair.* Under the traditional "defined contribution" approach, you cannot contribute a higher percentage of your earned income than the percentage of compensation you are contributing for participating employees. We are talking about percentages, not dollars. If you earn $40,000 and your paraprofessional assistant earns $7,500, you can contribute 15 per cent of each amount to a qualified Keogh plan or a Keogh-like "simplified pension plan": $6,000 for yourself and $1,125 for your assistant. Despite the disparity in the dollar value of the contributions, you will have complied with the rule.

Another choice is open to you. Instead of fixing contributions as a percentage of earned income, you can create a "defined benefit plan." Choose your ideal retirement benefit—as much as 100 per cent of your average annual earnings for the three highest consecutive years, up to $84,525 (or even more, as the Treasury approves cost of living adjustments)—and contribute enough each year to fund that benefit for yourself and your participating employees.

4. *Deduct your contributions.* Within prescribed limits, Keogh contributions are tax-deductible. "Defined benefit" plans are creatures of actuarial science, with changes in money rates and mortality tables yielding different assumptions. For now, the benefit for each year of plan participation may not exceed a participant's compensation for that year (up to $50,000) multiplied by a percentage which varies with the participant's age:

AGE AT PARTICIPATION	PERCENTAGE
30 or less	6.5
35	5.4
40	4.4
45	3.6
50	3.0
55	2.5
60 or over	2.0

Defined contribution plans are much simpler: each year you may contribute and deduct up to 15 per cent of your earned income, or $7,500, whichever is less. (To prevent undue discrimination against your employees, the percentage limit may only be computed on your first $100,000 of annual compensation. If you earn more than $100,000, you would be required to contribute at least 7½ per cent of your employees' earnings to take a full $7,500 deduction for yourself.)

But note this Keogh quirk: if you are earning $40,000, we said you could put away 15 per cent or $6,000 in your tax-sheltered Keogh plan. If an employee earns $7,500, you know you've got to contribute 15 per cent of that salary as well, $1,125.

What if your earnings zoom to $100,000 next year? You'd be limited to a $7,500 deductible contribution for yourself. This amount would represent only 7½ per cent of your income, however, so you'd only need to contribute 7½ per cent of your eligible employees' earnings. Therefore, for an employee earning $7,500, you'd be required to contribute only $562.50. Although Keogh intends to benefit your help as much as yourself, only the percentages need to be fair; the amounts don't.

5. *Feel free to contribute even more than you can deduct.* You can contribute another 10 per cent of earned income or $2,500, whichever is less, as a "voluntary" contribution. "Voluntary" contributions are not tax-deductible, but they are very much worth considering. Why? All that is contributed will be tax-sheltered, as we will see.

You say only your spouse works with you? If the spouse is paid a salary, you will both be able to make "voluntary" contributions up to the maximum.

[See §7.01]   6. *Create a tax shelter.* Once you make your contributions—deductible and "voluntary"—they will multiply. Select the investment approach that sounds best for you. Some of your choices are listed below.

[See §6.07]   (a) U.S. Retirement Plan Bonds are certainly safest. They pay 6 per cent interest, compounded semiannually, but cannot afford you much protection against inflation.

[See §12.08]   (b) Virtually all the major insurance companies offer life insurance and annuity programs, guaranteeing specific dollar payouts years from now. What those dollars will be worth then, of course, we cannot predict.

[See §6.02]   (c) You may be willing to take the risk and dabble in the market. Through a bank custodian or other trustee, you can buy shares in an investment company and, with luck, you might enjoy a healthier-than-average return on your investment.

What if you become dissatisfied with your choice? Once you elect an investment vehicle, are you locked into it? Probably not. Unless your plan expressly prohibits a switch, just transfer the net proceeds of your present plan to the plan you prefer. Usually, an amendment to the first plan and a transfer agreement will suffice.

Sometimes a transfer means termination or liquidation charges. To avoid them, you can "freeze" your plan—discontinue funding it—and make your future contributions to the plan you would prefer. Whether you transfer or "freeze," you might be raising some hidden legal issues, so let your lawyer handle the paperwork.

However you choose to invest—conservatively or aggressively—you will be establishing an enviable tax shelter. All the interest, dividends, and gains your plan generates will not be taxable to you when earned. Even they can be invested and reinvested, entirely free of federal income tax, so long as your plan continues.

At retirement—ordinarily between the ages of 59½ and 70½—you might elect to receive your benefits over a period of years and pay your income tax only as you receive these payments. You might prefer to receive your benefits all at once, though. If the latter, you may treat that portion of your distribution attributable to contributions made before 1974 as long-term capital gain, and that portion attributable to contributions made after 1973 as ordinary income. Capital gain treatment is only available, however, if you've participated in the plan for at least five years and elect the "ten-year averaging" computation for the ordinary income. "Ten-year averaging" works this way: add one-tenth of your ordinary taxable distribution to your other income for the year; then compute the tax on the one-tenth distribution and multiply that amount by ten. In large measure, you will avoid the high tax rates that apply to high incomes under our progressive tax system.

§2.03

AN ILLUSTRATION

Indisputably, Keogh plans are wonderful tax-cutters. A hypothetical example should prove the point: let's say you're in the 50 per cent tax bracket and you file a joint tax return with your spouse. Before taxes, you have $12,500 available to invest for your retirement. After you have paid your federal income tax, only $6,250 remains available for investment.

Assume that your investment dollars grow at the rate of 6 per cent a year, with those earnings being taxed all along at the 50 per cent bracket. For simplicity's sake, we will say that your other taxable income equals your deductions and exemptions. The net after-tax value of your first-year contribution, distributed to you as a lump sum, will have climbed to $15,184 after thirty years.

With the same dollars to invest at the same rate of interest, a Keogh plan can lead to a far happier result. Of your $12,500 available for investment before taxes, $10,000 remains available after taxes. That includes your $7,500 deductible contribution and your $2,500 nondeductible "voluntary" contribution made with after-tax dollars. Earnings on the full $10,000 accumulate tax-free every year. By the time you retire thirty years from now, your first-year contribution will be worth $57,435! Even after you pay your income tax on that lump-sum distribution, you'll still have as much as $47,922, assuming ten-year averaging.

§2.04

HOW MUCH SHOULD YOU CONTRIBUTE?

Undeniably, a Keogh plan is a wise way to save money. As a sole proprietor or a partner, you may be tempted to contribute all you can deduct and a substantial "voluntary" contribution too. Don't feel that you must, however. Contribute only what you really can afford, and you will still enjoy the rewards of systematic, tax-favored investing. In fact, you may want to set your plan up on a profit-sharing basis, so you can withhold contributions when your practice warrants it.

Contribute realistically, bearing in mind that excess contributions aren't deductible and are subject to a nondeductible 6 per cent cumulative excise tax. Since Keogh contributions can now be made any time before your federal income tax return is due (including any extension of time), you'll want to decide exactly how much to contribute only after you've seen the previous year's financial reports.

§2.05

THE IRA ALTERNATIVE

One last retirement wrinkle: proprietors and partners who see merit in funding a tax-sheltered retirement trust, but aren't about to do the same for all their three-year employees, should explore Keogh-like individual retirement accounts (IRAs). If you aren't participating in other qualified plans, you may contribute and deduct "above the line" up to 15 per cent of your own compensation (including earned income), but not more than $1,500. Participants with nonworking spouses may contribute up to $1,750 to an IRA with a spousal subaccount, or $875 to a separate account established for a nonworking spouse. Contributions are made to qualifying investment trusts or custodial accounts, or may be used to purchase approved annuities or retirement bonds. Earnings are tax-free until retirement (between the ages of 59½ and 70½), death, or disability. Then distributions, although taxed as ordinary income, may allow you to average your income and pay less tax.

§2.06

THE EFFECT OF KEOGH AND IRA

Rational contributions to a Keogh or IRA plan can defer income taxes today and provide you with a secure retirement tomorrow. Let one of them work for you.

CHAPTER 3

GOING CORPORATE:
What It's All About

§3.01

TAX SHELTERS GALORE

Health professionals who choose to practice in the corporate form enjoy tax benefits unknown to their colleagues who continue to render professional services as sole proprietors or partners. If you set up your own professional corporation, you will be creating a brand-new taxable entity. You will be an employee of a duly established corporation to which all of your patients will pay your fees directly. The corporation, not you, will be obliged to pay a tax on all the fees earned less its deductions, including your salary. These deductions may very well leave your corporation with no taxable income at all. Consequently, the only tax you may pay will be on the compensation you earn as an employee. As a result, you will reduce your tax bite.

That is the major premise, and it is loaded with opportunities. These are a few worth exploring:

1. The corporation is not only a new taxpayer; it is also a new investor, and a privileged one at that. It can passively invest in other corporations and earn dividend income, 85 per cent exempt from federal income tax. That which is taxed is subject to a substantially lower rate than you pay on your individual investment earnings. Compare these typical results:

	YOUR STOCK INVESTMENT			*YOUR CORPORATION'S STOCK INVESTMENT*	
Dividend income	$1000			$1000	
Dividend exclusion	100 (the limit)	$100		850	$850
Taxable income	$ 900			$ 150	
The tax	− 450 (at 50%)	+ 450		− 30 (at 20%)	+ 120
Net after taxes		$550			$970

2. Your professional corporation can accumulate at least $150,000 of practice and investment earnings without a penalty and without your being personally taxed on it. Of course, you will be taxed on any income you actually receive as salary. Contrast that with your tax status as a sole proprietor or partner, though. Today,

you have to pay a tax on all the income your practice earns, or on your proportionate share of partnership income, whether or not it is paid out to you.

3. Your corporation can generally contribute as much as 15 per cent of corporate salaries to a qualified profit-sharing plan. These contributions are periodically made to a trust, which invests them on behalf of the corporation's employees, including you. The corporation can deduct the full amount it contributes, yet you and your staff realize no income that is taxable at present. Moreover, the money the trust earns is tax-free as well. [See Chapter 4]

Most important, the income you receive from your corporate retirement plan is taxable only as you receive it, and at a very favorable rate. Since you will probably be in a much lower tax bracket after you retire, you will realize a much greater portion of retirement plan benefits as "real" income. The government's thinking behind all these tax savings is to help the corporation's employees, not its owners. Remember, though, you will be your corporation's No. 1 employee.

4. Your professional corporation can also offer you a pension plan. As mentioned above, a qualified profit-sharing plan allows your corporation to contribute periodically a tax-sheltered share of its profits for the benefit of its employees, who ultimately receive these profits and their fruits in a tax-sheltered way. A pension plan works the other way around. Here, the benefits you and the other employees will receive at retirement are determined in advance, and your corporation periodically contributes to the plan whatever funds are necessary to realize those benefits for you. Benefits can and do differ from employee to employee; they are a function of age, sex, length of service, and duties, so your plan can reflect your own needs and wants provided they are economically rational and nondiscriminatory. [See Chapter 4]

5. The larger professional corporation may provide up to $50,000 worth of group term life insurance for its employees, you among them. The cost is tax-deductible by your corporation and not reportable as income on your personal tax return. [See §12.04]

An illustration should underscore just how cost-effective a benefit that can be:

UNINCORPORATED YOU		AFTER YOU INCORPORATE, THE CORPORATION	YOU
Your $50,000 term policy may cost	$400	$400	$0
A $15,000 policy for an employee may cost		100	0
(you wouldn't buy it)	0		
The tax you'd pay to clear that much	400 (at 50%)	0	0
Total outlay	$800	$500	$0

6. Any employee may enter into an agreement with the corporation to defer receiving part of his or her salary until later in life. Some of the income you earn now can be paid to you after retirement, when you'll be in a lower tax bracket. [See §12.02]

7. The hospital and medical expenses of employees and their dependents, including you and your family, can be paid by insurance plans funded by the corporation, and these payments are tax-free.

Another example to prove the point: suppose your practice nets $60,000. You spend $500 in insurance premiums each year, $1,500 in uninsured dental and medical bills, and $400 for drugs—a total of $2,400. Contrast the net-dollars effect on your practice before and after incorporation.

	UNINCORPORATED YOU		AFTER YOU INCORPORATE, THE CORPORATION	YOU
Net income	$60,000		$60,000	
Medical expense	(2,400)			
Deductions:				
-insurance		$150 (the statutory maximum)	$ 500	$0
-medical		0 (since they're less than 3% of your adjusted gross income)	1,500	0
-drugs		0 (since they're less than 1% of your adjusted gross income)	400	0
Total deductions	$150		$2,400	$0
Tax on nondeductible medical expense (at 50% bracket)	(1,125)		(0)	
Net	$56,475		$57,600 (available for distribution as your salary)	

8. The corporation can pay the surviving spouse of any employee up to $5,000 as a death benefit and deduct it. The spouse receives payment tax-free.
9. Finally, let's not underestimate the effect of all these extra benefits on your staff's morale.

§3.02

AN ILLUSTRATION

Let's assume a few things about you:

1. Your age is 40.
2. Your professional practice nets $50,000 annually.
3. You have no retirement or health plan.
4. You file a joint tax return with your spouse and declare no personal deductions or additional dependency exemptions.

Your federal income tax is $14,778, leaving you with $35,222 in spendable income.

Now, suppose you incorporate. You will have no net income from your practice; instead, you will have a salary. You might draw $3,000 a month or $36,000 a year. You will place, for example, $9,000 in a retirement plan for yourself and use $5,000 to pay your health costs and make them deductible. Instead of paying $14,778 on your $50,000 income, you pay only $8,506 and can pocket the difference. That's $6,272 every year. If you're 40 years old now, in 25 years you will have saved $156,800.

TODAY'S PERSONAL PRACTICE

Your professional fees	$50,000	
LESS:		
Your salary	-(0)-	
Your retirement plan	-(0)-	
Your health costs	-(0)-	
Your taxable personal income	$50,000	
LESS:		
Your personal income tax	14,778	$14,778
Your take-home income	$35,222	

TOMORROW'S CORPORATE PRACTICE

Your corporation's fees	$50,000	
LESS:		
Your salary	(36,000)	
Your retirement plan	(9,000)	
Your health costs	(5,000)	
Your taxable corporate income	-0-	
PLUS: Your salary	$36,000	
LESS: Your personal income tax	8,506	8,506
Your take-home income	$27,494	
Your annual tax saving		$ 6,272

§3.03

STILL MORE BENEFITS

It is clear that professional incorporation may offer you a world of tax benefits and some other advantages as well. Any corporation affords its stockholders these pluses:

- *Continuity of life.* A corporation never dies. It has a life of its own that goes on uninterrupted after the death of its owners. It follows that once you incorporate, it will be easier to acquire good associates. [See §12.02]

- *Free transferability of interests.* When the time comes to transfer ownership, corporate stock can be sold without the consent of other owners. Compare that with the lot of one who practices as a partner: he cannot sell his interest until the permission of all the other partners is obtained. [See §1.02]

- *Centralized management.* Authority is *structured*, with responsibility for corporate decision-making generally concentrated in the president. Since relationships must be formalized, your rights and obligations no longer will be left to casual understandings or chance.

- *Limited liability.* In a partnership, every partner is liable for the negligence of all the other partners. If you become a corporate shareholder-employee, however, in most states, you will be liable only for your own negligence.

§3.04

WHO SHOULDN'T INCORPORATE?

So far, incorporating seems like the ideal mode of professional practice. You can cut your income tax, build up your retirement investments with tax-sheltered dollars, and conduct a practice underpinned by a set of sound business principles. A professional corporation is not for everyone, though. If any of the following examples describes your practice, by all means don't incorporate:

[See §2.02 and Chapter 4]

- *Earnings are much less than $50,000.* You cannot shelter income that you spend. Under these circumstances, a corporate retirement program, probably the single greatest motivation to incorporate, will not serve you any better than the Keogh plan, which you can enjoy without the bother and expense of incorporating.
- *Difficulty maintaining records.* Once incorporated, you must maintain accurate and thorough books. Your practice will become a governmentally regulated business entity. You can make the most of your preferential tax treatment only if you can review your fiscal year at tax time and know exactly what deductible expenses your corporation incurred.
- *Likelihood of large temporary expenses.* If your child has just started college or if your mother may require surgery soon, this may be the wrong time for you to incorporate. You ought to be able to predict with some certainty what your financial picture will look like a year from now.
- *Difficulty conforming to the rules.* Your share of the corporation's income will be yours *eventually*, but not necessarily as it is earned. If you cannot trust yourself to keep your hands out of petty cash, or if you do not like the idea of being restricted to a fixed salary, the corporate life style is not for you.

§3.05

THE FORMALITIES

If you have not been dissuaded, see your attorney. Corporate law is a maze requiring expert guidance at every stage. Should your lawyer agree that incorporation is the right move for you, here are some of the things you and he will need to accomplish together:

1. Skillfully draft and properly file your Articles of Incorporation.
2. Get a Charter.
3. Issue stock.
4. Publish bylaws.
5. Hold shareholders' meetings initially and at least annually.
6. Hold directors' meetings initially and at least annually.
7. Enter into an employment agreement with your corporation.
8. Change the name on your office door to indicate the full corporate name.
9. Change your letterhead.
10. Change your billhead.
11. Change your professional cards.
12. Revise your telephone listing.
13. Revise any listings in professional directories.
14. Obtain a federal Employer's Identification Number from the Internal Revenue Service.
15. Open a new bank account in the corporation's name after it has been authorized at your first directors' meeting.

16. Consider transferring any loans you've obtained in the course of your practice to the corporation, which then would assume them.
17. Assign to the corporation any leases on office furniture and existing professional equipment.
18. Acquire malpractice, workmen's compensation, and other insurance coverage on all employees—including yourself—in the corporate name.

Remember, if the IRS concludes that yours is a "sham" corporation, all the tax benefits of incorporation may be lost and all your effort will have been in vain.

§3.06

A CONCLUSION OR TWO

The demands your corporation will make may easily be overbalanced by all the tax advantages and fringe benefits that have tantalized corporate executives for decades and only recently have become available to professionals. Yet, the ultimate decision to form a corporation can only be made after serious deliberation and discussion with legal counsel. For now, we can safely conclude that if you are content to live as a corporate employee and have an income to justify it, a professional corporation may very well be worth your effort.

CHAPTER 4

GOING CORPORATE:
All You Need To Know About Profit-Sharing and Pension Plans

§4.01

HOW TO USE RETIREMENT PLANS

Thousands who have "gone corporate" have done so primarily to enjoy the many advantages of "qualified" retirement plans. After all, deferred compensation is good business: it helps attract competent employees, who will always be in short supply; it boosts employee morale and, with it, productivity; it reduces employee turnover. Possibly most important, it is an effective tax-avoidance tool.

§4.02

SOME TAX TIPS

Here is how the IRS will look at your corporate retirement plan:

- Your corporation can deduct all the contributions it makes.
- Corporate employees, you included, do not realize any taxable income until retirement benefits are distributed, presumably when lower tax rates will apply.
- That is also true for the income corporate contributions earn.
- For employees who have not contributed to the plan, benefits will be taxed just as ordinary income is, but lump-sum distributions are special. First, that portion allocable to an employee's own contributions is recovered tax-free. Next, that portion allocable to pre-1974 plan participation years may be taxed as long-term capital gain. Finally, the balance is taxed as ordinary income and may be eligible for ten-year averaging.
- If you'd prefer, the whole distribution may be treated as ordinary income subject to ten-year averaging.
- A beneficiary of a deceased employee may apply the special lump-sum rules and claim a $5,000 death benefit too.
- The proceeds can be "rolled over" to an IRA within 60 days, allowing you to defer taxation entirely.

Table 4–1 HOW A CORPORATE RETIREMENT PLAN SAVES TAX DOLLARS

	A CORPORATION WITHOUT A PLAN	A SOLE PROPRIETOR OR A PARTNER WITH A KEOGH PLAN	A CORPORATION WITH A PLAN
Your gross income	$50,000	$ 50,000	$ 50,000
Contributions		7,000	10,000 (a reasonable contribution)
Taxable income	$50,000 (distributed as salary)	$ 43,000	$ 40,000 (distributed as salary)
Your personal income tax (assuming you file jointly)	$14,778	$ 11,516	$ 10,226
Your savings:		3,262	4,552
After 10 years:		$ 32,620	$ 45,520
After 20 years:		$ 65,240	$ 91,040
After 30 years:		$ 97,860	$136,560

§4.03

"QUALIFYING" YOUR PLAN

The deferral of personal income taxes and the tax-free accumulation of investment dollars are the goals of any employee benefit plan. Your plan must "qualify" for the privileges it seeks, however. You must prove that you will be providing your employees with real retirement security. Meeting these statutory requirements and complying with all kinds of reporting obligations imposed by the Employee Retirement Income Security Act will lead to qualification and substantial tax savings:

1. In the first place, your plan must be a deferred compensation plan.
2. It must be permanent.
3. Your plan must be in written form and communicated to employees.
4. If a trust is being established to receive and invest contributions, the trust instrument ought to be in writing too.
5. The plan must be created for the exclusive benefit of the corporation's employees and their beneficiaries, but that includes you, of course.
6. You are not supposed to discriminate in favor of shareholder-employees, that is, yourself and your colleagues. Contributions and benefits, however, may vary with salary and years of service. Age limits and waiting periods can be imposed as well.

    In addition, if you integrate the plan with Social Security benefits, you can shift benefits away from anyone who earns less than a prescribed salary, and toward yourself.
7. Your plan must benefit 70 per cent or more of the corporation's full-time employees. Alternatively, 70 per cent must be eligible to participate, and 80 per cent of those eligible must actually do so.
8. Benefits must *vest*—that is, employees must become irrevocably entitled to them within a certain period of time—certainly at the end of ten years, and sometimes sooner.

§4.04

PREPARE FOR THE WORST

No doubt you will strive to meet these requirements. However, what if your plan does not qualify? What if it qualifies and then loses that privileged status?

- The corporation will get its tax deduction for the contributions it makes only if the participants' rights are *nonforfeitable* when the contributions are made. Otherwise, there will be no deduction at all for the corporation.
- Employees will be taxed immediately on nonforfeitable contributions made on their behalf. Forfeitable contributions will become taxable when benefits are distributed.
- Most nonqualified plans provide for the immediate payment of benefits, so there is no opportunity to build up tax-exempt income.

The Internal Revenue Service, the Department of Labor, and the Pension Benefit Guarantee Corporation are forever redefining retirement plan guidelines. Your attorney will guide you through the maze of applicable legislation and administrative pronouncements. Protect yourself by acting swiftly. As soon as your plan is adopted, have your lawyer seek Treasury approval. If it is denied, you may be able to amend your plan immediately and maximize its value. One provision that is highly recommended is that the initial payments made by the corporation be returned if approval cannot be obtained.

§4.05

PENSION VERSUS PROFIT-SHARING

When you set out your plan's provisions, you and your lawyer will work hard at complying with federal guidelines. You will also give serious thought to the often-puzzling question, just what kind of a retirement plan is ideal for our corporation?

Plans are generally grouped into two types—*defined-benefit pension* and *defined-contribution profit-sharing*. Pension plans are calculated to provide employees with determinable benefits after retirement; contributions are actuarially computed at least annually to assure the ultimate payment of desired benefits. Profit-sharing plans, on the other hand, have the corporation contribute a share of its profits for the benefit of a designated group of employees. At retirement, all employees are entitled to their share of the fund. Along with corporate contributions, a plan may require participating employees to make contributions of up to 6 per cent of their pay. Beyond this, employees may voluntarily contribute as much as 10 per cent of covered pay. These voluntary contributions will also gain tax-favored treatment.

Your professional corporation may choose to institute a pension plan, a profit-sharing plan, or both. Select a plan that fits your practice on the basis of these factors:

1. *How old are you?* Profit-sharing plans favor younger employees. The more years you work for your corporation, the longer you share in its profits. Prospective years of service are not so important in the pension plan context; a pension plan will set your eventual benefits today and continually adjust corporate contributions to arrive at your goal years from now.
2. *Do you want corporate contributions to depend on profit?* By definition, profit-sharing plans do; pension plans do not.
3. *Do you want to retain discretion in making contributions?* Profit-sharing plans are usually formulated to allow corporate directors decision-making flexibility in this regard. Pension plans leave the fixing of contributions to the actuaries.

4. *How much do you want your corporation to contribute?* Contributions in profit-sharing plans are limited to a maximum of 15 per cent of the annual corporate payroll. No such maximum applies to deferred-benefit pension plans.

5. *Do you want the corporation to be able to recover excess contributions?* A profit-sharing plan cannot—ever. Once monies have been earmarked as the corporation's contributed share of profit, they are unalterably a part of the fund. If participants leave the corporate employ before their interests vest, their contributions are divided among the remaining participating employees. If there's an actuarial error in a pension plan, however, excess contributions can be recovered when the plan ends, and forfeited contributions serve to decrease the corporation's future contribution requirements.

6. *What fringe benefits do you want to include?* Profit-sharing plans can include [See §12.11] health and accident insurance, but pension plans cannot. At best, they can include a disability pension benefit.

We have seen the exciting Keogh opportunities for sole proprietors and partners. A corporate plan can do much more for you, mostly because structuring possibilities beyond the classical forms are much greater. A brief summary of retirement plan alternatives is shown in Table 4–2.

§4.06

USING A TRUST

Once you decide on the form of your plan, how will it operate? The typical retirement plan creates a trust, empowered to receive corporate and sometimes employee contributions and to invest them in the manner the trust agreement defines. All that is earned accumulates tax-free for the benefit of all participating employees. The trust is a separate entity in which employees' retirement dollars can grow under the strictest of fiduciary safeguards. That is why certain trust transactions are prohibited by law:

- The trust cannot make loans unless they are adequately secured, and a reasonable rate of interest must be received.
- The only compensation the trust may pay is a reasonable amount for services actually rendered.
- The trust cannot buy stock or make any other purchase for more than "adequate consideration."
- It can't sell any major asset for less than "adequate consideration."
- Finally, plan assets other than insurance contracts must be held in a trust run by a bank, insurance carrier, or bonded fiduciary. The trustee is charged with managing trust funds for the benefit of all participants as a "prudent individual" would, diversifying the investments and avoiding questionable transactions with himself or herself, the corporation, and its management.

§4.07

THE GOAL

The plan you and your counsel design will generate a well-protected retirement fund. All at once, you will serve the goals of sound personnel management, creative tax avoidance, and personal retirement planning. A corporate retirement plan just might help solve more than one problem that's been plaguing you.

Table 4–2 RETIREMENT PLAN POSSIBILITIES

		HOW MUCH TO CONTRIBUTE	WHAT HAPPENS WHEN AN EMPLOYEE LEAVES YOU	WHERE EACH YEAR'S INVESTMENT GAINS AND LOSSES GO	YOUR RETIREMENT ACCOUNT
Defined-contribution plan	Money-purchase	Up to 15% of earned income, to a maximum of $7,500	Takes his account balance along	Adjust account balances	The balance of your account
Defined-benefit plan	Fixed-benefit	In accordance with IRS actuarial tables	Takes his account balance along	Increase or reduce your annual contribution	Pre-established amount based on your age at plan's inception, usually less than $5,000 a year
Defined-contribution plans	Profit-sharing	Discretionary; up to 15% of compensation, to a maximum of $28,175 (or more as inflation justifies)	Balance is forfeited to remaining partici-pants' accounts	Adjust account balances	The balance of your account
	Money-purchase	Fixed; up to 25% of compensation, to a maximum of $28,175 (or more as inflation justifies)	Balance reduces future corporate contributions	Adjust account balances	The balance of your account
	Profit-sharing/Money-purchase combo	Partly discretionary, partly fixed; up to 25% of compensation, to a maximum of $28,175 (or more as inflation justifies)	If contributions are at the maximum, balance reduces future corporate contribu-tions; otherwise, balance is forfeited to remaining partici-pants' accounts	Adjust account balances	The balance of your account

KEOGH CHOICES

CORPORATE CHOICES

Defined-benefit plans	Target-benefit	What's needed to fund a pre-established benefit, up to 25% of compensation or $28,175 (or more as inflation justifies)	Balance reduces future corporate contributions	Adjust account balances	Pre-established benefit, up to 100% of compensation, a maximum of $84,524 plus or minus investment results (or more as inflation justifies)
	Fixed-benefit	What's needed to fund a pre-established benefit, up to 25% of compensation or $28,175 (or more as inflation justifies)	Balance reduces future corporate contributions	Increase or reduce corporate contributions	Pre-established benefit, up to 100% of compensation; maximum of $84,524, (or more as inflation justifies)
Combination plan	Money-purchase & Fixed-benefit	Fixed, up to 10% of compensation	Balance reduces future corporate contributions	Adjust account balances	The balance of your account pre-established benefit, up to 100% of compensation; maximum of $84,524 (or more as inflation justifies)
		What's needed to fund a pre-established benefit, with no ceiling	Balance reduces future corporate contributions	Increase or reduce corporate contributions	

CHAPTER 5

TRIMMING YOUR
INCOME TAX

§5.01

**WHERE WE ARE HEADED AND WHAT YOU
CAN DO ABOUT IT**

Our federal income tax laws are so much in a state of transition that whatever tax strategy you see recommended here really ought to be considered only after you have read this morning's newspaper. Taxes are forever escalating, and the system's injustices are forever coming to the fore. In response, the public is challenging virtually every major tax assumption. So, Caveat Number One must insist, heed the reform that is in the wings. Check with your lawyer *today* before adopting any suggestion. You will surely need a lawyer's help to implement most far-reaching ideas anyway—and to cite the "whole law," not just the shorthand rules you will find here.

Here are some changes in the offing and, bearing Caveat Number One in mind, what you might do about them now:

[See Chapter 7]   1. Recent Internal Revenue Service action has destroyed tax shelter after tax shelter. Choose your investments on the basis of their safety, growth, and income rather than their tax loss potential. That's more than just good tax advice.

[See §5.06]   2. Congress is now seriously considering reducing the amounts you can deduct for gifts to charity. Today, individuals can generally deduct contributions to public charities in amounts up to half their adjusted gross income. Take advantage of the temporary state of the law and make your contributions mean the most on your next tax return. If you are going to give, give now.

[See §6.02]   3. Married couples who file joint returns can exclude up to $200 in stock dividends from their taxable incomes. The dividend exclusion is coming under fire, however. Now may be a good time to consider selling your dividend-paying stock and buying growth issues instead.

[See §5.04]   4. You can limit the tax payable on a capital gains income by holding your investment for a year or more. Only 40% the excess of net long-term capital gain over net-short term capital loss is taxed at regular rates. The whole capital gains idea is being questioned, however. You will probably see another gain tax overhaul soon. Keep congressional thinking in mind as you reevaluate your investment portfolio.

§5.02

"ADJUST" YOUR INCOME DOWN TO SIZE

Planning is a must. Any tax strategy is intended to shave your gross income in every legitimate way. Start with "adjustments," those privileged expenses that prune your gross income even before you start itemizing your "personal" deductions. These "adjustments" in particular will be of interest to the self-employed professional:

1. Moving expenses. If you move 35 miles farther from your old home than your old job was, to begin working for yourself, or if you change your place of self-employment by 35 miles or more, you might be able to deduct your moving expenses, even the cost of driving there. What's more, you can deduct up to $3,000 for:
   a. House-hunting expenses.
   b. A month's stay at temporary lodging until your new home is ready for you.
   c. The cost of selling or leasing your old home and buying or leasing your new one. The Revenue Code is very specific about these points, so have your lawyer explain the technicalities.
2. Travel expenses. Do you travel between hospitals or offices during the course of your professional day? Do you make house calls? If so, you can probably deduct travel costs. The accepted estimate is 17¢ a mile for the first 15,000, 10¢ a mile over 15,000, plus parking lot charges and tolls, of course.
3. Keogh plan or IRA contributions. [See Chapter 2]
4. Most accountants' and lawyers' fees.
5. Bonuses to employees.
6. Depreciation. [See §5.11]
7. Entertainment expense.
8. Interest on "business debts."
9. Liability insurance, unemployment insurance, and workmen's compensation insurance. [See §§12.09 and 12.10]
10. Office rent, utilities, and telephone charges.
11. Salaries and wages.
12. Professional association dues.

§5.03

"ADJUSTING" AS AN EMPLOYEE

What if you are not self-employed? As an employee, you can deduct these adjustments, among others:

1. Travel and entertainment expenses, if you are away from home, pursuing the goals of your practice.
2. Expenses your employer reimburses, offsetting the reimbursement which must be reported as part of your Gross Income.
3. Moving expenses. If you move in order to assume a new position 35 miles away or even to continue working for the same employer, you may be entitled to deduct your moving expenses.
4. IRA contributions.

§5.04

THREE MORE ADJUSTMENTS

Whether you are an employer or an employee, do not pass over these adjustments:

[See §5.01]
1. Long-term capital gains. Deduct 60 per cent of the excess of long-term capital gains over short-term capital losses.
2. Losses in the sale of any investment or business property.
3. Alimony paid.

§5.05

THE IMPORT OF AGI

Once you have deducted all the adjustments you can, you are left with your *Adjusted Gross Income* (AGI). From that amount, you deduct still more to compute your *Taxable Income*—the final figure against which your tax is computed.

If your Taxable Income is the important number in determining your tax liability, why all the talk about that intermediate calculation, Adjusted Gross Income? Whether a deduction is labeled a deduction "*for* Adjusted Gross Income" or one "*from* Adjusted Gross Income" can tremendously influence the final result and your whole relationship with the Internal Revenue Service. Here's why:

1. Deductions "for AGI" are yours even if you don't itemize deductions in excess of the "zero bracket amount" (to be discussed later).
2. You can deduct your family's medical expenses only to the extent they exceed 3 per cent of your AGI and the cost of medicines only to the extent it exceeds 1 per cent of your AGI.
3. You can usually deduct up to 20 per cent of your AGI for contributions to private foundations, and up to 50 per cent for contributions to public charities.
4. If your AGI is less than $10,000, you may be entitled to a refundable *earned income credit*, the controversial "negative income tax."

§5.06

ITEMIZE ALL YOU CAN

Federal income tax tables now reflect a tax-free "zero bracket amount." The "zero bracket amount"—$3,400 on a joint return—replaces the old standard deduction and low income allowance, and for most taxpayers allows more tax-free income. Only itemized deductions beyond the "zero bracket amount" are separately deducted.

Many itemized deductions will come to mind immediately. These may not:

[See §12.11]
1. *Medical expenses.* First, you can deduct half your premiums for medical care insurance, up to $150. As for your other medical expenses, they must exceed 3 per cent of your AGI if they are to be claimed. Do not forget the cost of transportation to get medical treatment; 7¢ a mile is an often-accepted guesstimate.

[See §5.01]
2. *Charitable contributions.* A significant tax benefit is yours if you make a donation to a recognized public charity, especially if you donate certain appreciated property you have held for more than a year. Not only can you deduct the fair market value of your gift but also you can avoid paying a tax on the appreciation. The effective cost of your donation plummets while your tax deduction jumps. Watch out, though, because even the minds of seasoned lawyers boggle at the complex patchwork of subtleties this area of the law offers.
3. *Interest.* Any interest you pay on your own debt is usually deductible. In fact, it can be deductible for AGI if it is incurred in your profession. Otherwise, interest is usually an itemized deduction. When totalling the interest you pay during the

year, remember you can deduct the finance charges on your revolving charge accounts, if charges are added to any unpaid balance each month.

One caveat: your "investment interest" deduction is generally limited to $10,000 plus your "net investment income." This, of course, is a restriction aimed squarely at highly leveraged tax shelter investments.

4. *Taxes.* Some kind of taxes are income tax-deductible if they are imposed on you and if you pay them during the tax year. They include these:

a. Customs duties
b. Federal excise taxes
c. Federal Social Security taxes
d. Federal unemployment insurance taxes
e. State unemployment insurance contributions
f. State disability taxes
g. State and local property taxes
h. State and city income taxes
i. Some state sales taxes
j. Local special assessments, but only if they're made for maintenance purposes or to pay interest obligations

5. *Personal casualty losses*, except the first $100 of loss from each nonbusiness casualty.

§5.07

YOU KNOW YOUR SPOUSE AND KIDS WILL HELP

One more deduction category, and you will know your Taxable Income: dependency exemptions. You can deduct $1,000 for every exemption. You are allowed an exemption for yourself, one for your spouse, and one for each of your dependents. A taxpayer 65 or older can add another exemption; a blind person still another. Those exemptions for age and blindness are available for spouses as well.

§5.08

GIVING YOURSELF CREDIT

Thus we arrive at your Taxable Income and your tax computation, but don't put your pencil down yet. You may be eligible for one or more credits against your tax. Consider these:

- A 10 per cent investment tax credit is allowed for qualified investment property in the first year it's placed in use.
- A $50 ($100 for joint returns) credit may be taken for half your eligible political and "newsletter fund" contributions.
- Persons 65 or over may take a credit equal to 15 per cent of their income up to $3,750 (on joint returns with both spouses 65 and over), reduced by Social Security and other pensions excludable from gross income, and by one-half the excess of their AGI over $10,000 (if they file a joint return).
- A child and dependent care credit is available to taxpayers who furnish more than half the cost of maintaining a household which includes one or more qualifying individuals,

and incur creditable expenses for services to enable them to be gainfully employed. The credit is 20 per cent of those expenses paid during the year, up to $2,000 if one and $4,000 if two or more individuals qualify. And now, payments to grandparents for care of their grandchildren may qualify for the child-care credit.

• A 20 per cent work incentive credit is allowed for wages paid to certain employees certified by the Secretary of Labor under the Work Incentive Program and to certain welfare recipients under the Aid to Dependent Children Program. Generally, the credit ceiling is the taxpayer's regular tax liability up to $50,000, and half his or her regular tax liability above $50,000.

§5.09

A SUMMARY

How the tax laws affect you ought to make some sense to you now. You start with Gross Income—your fees or salary and any other reportable income. From these you "adjust" by deducting those special expenses that are recorded on line 28 of your Form 1040. The difference is Adjusted Gross Income—the magical number that's used to calculate how much you can deduct for medical expenses and charitable contributions. All kinds of "personal" deductions beyond your zero bracket amount are then subtracted from AGI, and so are your dependency exemptions. The result is Taxable Income, the amount that directly determines your tax, and all kinds of credits can ease the pain.

§5.10

HOW SCHEDULE C LOOKS

If you practice solo, the crux of your return is Schedule C. Schedule C spells out the "Profit (or Loss) From Business or Profession"—in short, how your tax year fared in dollars and cents. With some background behind us, let us zero in on Schedule C and see how tax theory applies to your practice. A line-by-line commentary should give you some ideas come next April. (You'll find examples on the following pages.)

Line A: Obviously, your principal "business" activity is performing services as a health professional. Be sure to specify your discipline.

Line B: Enter any name under which you operate your practice, such as Internal Medicine Center.

Line C: Take note. The IRS is not asking your Social Security number again, but the special number assigned you as an employer.

Line D: Record your *office* address.

Line E: Almost all health professionals are *cash-basis* taxpayers. That way, you pay a tax on income only after it is received. As an *accrual-basis* taxpayer, you

**SCHEDULE C
(Form 1040)**
Department of the Treasury
Internal Revenue Service

Profit or (Loss) From Business or Profession
(Sole Proprietorship)
Partnerships, Joint Ventures, etc., Must File Form 1065.
► Attach to Form 1040.   ► See Instructions for Schedule C (Form 1040).

19__

Name of proprietor	Tax Conscious Practitioner	Social security number 135 79 0246

A Principal business activity (see Schedule C Instructions) ► Physician ; product ► Services

B Business name ► Does not apply

C Employer identification number ► 99-1111111

D Business address (number and street) ► 123 Main Street

City, State and ZIP code ► Williams Point, New York 12180

C

		Yes	No
E Indicate method of accounting: (1) ☒ Cash (2) ☐ Accrual (3) ☐ Other ►			
F Was an Employer's Quarterly Federal Tax Return, Form 941, filed for this business for any quarter in 19..?		✓	
G Did you own the business at the end of 19..?		✓	

H How many months in 19.. did you own this business? ► 12

I Check valuation method(s) used for total closing inventory: ☐ cost, ☐ lower of cost or market, ☐ other (if "other," attach explanation).

Was there any substantial change in determining quantities, costs, or valuations between opening and closing inventory? If "Yes," attach explanation.

Income

1 Gross receipts or sales $50,500.00 Less: returns and allowances $500.00 .... Balance ►	1	50,000 00
2 Less: Cost of goods sold and/or operations (Schedule C–1, line 8)	2	-0-
3 Gross profit	3	50,000 00
4 Other income (attach schedule)	4	-0-
5 Total income (add lines 3 and 4)	5	50,000 00

Deductions

6 Depreciation (explain in Schedule C–2)	6	1,500 00
7 Taxes on business and business property	7	250 00
8 Rent on business property	8	2,400 00
9 Repairs	9	-0-
10 Salaries and wages not included on line 3, Schedule C–1 (exclude any paid to yourself)	10	7,200 00
11 Insurance	11	325 00
12 Legal and professional fees	12	900 00
13 Commissions	13	-0-
14 Amortization (attach statement)	14	-0-
15 a Pension and profit-sharing plans (see Schedule C Instructions)	15a	400 00
b Employee benefit programs (see Schedule C Instructions)	b	80 00
16 Interest on business indebtedness	16	50 00
17 Bad debts arising from sales or services	17	-0-
18 Depletion	18	-0-
19 Other business expenses (specify):		
a Telephone	120 00	
b Telephone answering service	60 00	
c Postage	100 00	
d Utilities	300 00	
e Professional journals	32 00	
f Professional supplies	540 00	
g Professional society dues	300 00	
h Office supplies	150 00	
i Auto expense	120	
j Miscellaneous	50 00	
k		
l		
m		
n		
o		
p Total other business expenses (add lines 19a through 19o)	19p	1,672 00
20 Total deductions (add lines 6 through 19p)	20	14,377 00
21 Net profit or (loss) (subtract line 20 from line 5). Enter here and on Form 1040, line 13. **ALSO** enter on Schedule SE, line 5a ►	21	35,723 00

Did you claim a deduction for expenses of an office in your home? ☐ Yes ☒ No

Schedule C (Form 1040) 1977   Page **2**

SCHEDULE C-1.—Cost of Goods Sold and/or Operations
(See Schedule C Instructions for Line 2)

1 Inventory at beginning of year (if different from last year's closing inventory, attach explanation) . . .	**1**	
2 Purchases $.................. Less: cost of items withdrawn for personal use $.................. **Balance ▶**	**2**	
3 Cost of labor (do not include salary paid to yourself)	**3**	
4 Materials and supplies	**4**	
5 Other costs (attach schedule)	**5**	
6 Add lines 1 through 5	**6**	
7 Inventory at end of year	**7**	
8 Cost of goods sold and/or operations (subtract line 7 from line 6). Enter here and on page 1, line 2 .	**8**	

SCHEDULE C-2.—Depreciation (See Schedule C Instructions for Line 6)
If you need more space, use Form 4562.

a. Description of property	b. Date acquired	c. Cost or other basis	d. Depreciation allowed or allowable in prior years	e. Method of computing depreciation	f. Life or rate	g. Depreciation for this year	
1 Total additional first-year depreciation (do not include in items below)————————▶						0	
2 Other depreciation:							
Furniture & fixtures	1-15-00	15,000	1,500	SL	10 yrs.	1,500	—
3 Totals		15,000		. . . . .		1,500	00
4 Depreciation claimed in Schedule C-1, above						-0-	
5 Balance (subtract line 4 from line 3). Enter here and on page 1, line 6						1,500	00

SCHEDULE C-3.—Expense Account Information (See Schedule C Instructions for Schedule C-3)

	Name	Expense account	Salaries and Wages	
Enter information with regard to yourself and your five highest paid employees. In determining the five highest paid employees, expense account allowances must be added to their salaries and wages. However, the information need not be submitted for any employee for whom the combined amount is less than $25,000, or for yourself if your expense account allowance plus line 21, page 1, is less than $25,000.	Owner		/////////	////
	1			
	2			
	3			
	4			
Did you claim a deduction for expenses connected with:	5			

(1) Entertainment facility (boat, resort, ranch, etc.)? . . ☐ Yes ☒ No   (3) Employees' families at conventions or meetings? . . . ☐ Yes ☒ No

(2) Living accommodations (except employees on business)? ☐ Yes ☒ No   (4) Employee or family vacations not reported on Form W-2? ☐ Yes ☒ No

would be required to pay a tax on any outstanding fee you have billed, even if your patient does not pay you by year's end.

Line F: You would check YES if you withheld income tax from wages, annuities, supplemental unemployment compensation benefits, and taxes under FICA.

Lines G
 and H: IRS wants to be able to trace the ownership of your practice.

Line I: Our Dr. Practitioner has no inventory on hand.

And getting down to the particulars:

Line 1: Report all you have received for services rendered, less any bad checks or other "returns and allowances." Do not report any gains on the sale of property used in your profession on Schedule C; that is what Schedule D and Form 4797 are for.

Line 2: You can cite your materials and supplies expense at this point. Many would argue it is preferable to list *all* your professional expenses on lines 6 to 19, where you can more uniformly demonstrate your cash outflow.

Line 3: This is just a summary statement.

Line 4: We will assume there is no other professional income.

Line 5: Here is another summary statement.

Line 6: Charge off your capital investment in property over the asset's useful life.

§5.11

THE DEPRECIATION STORY

The IRS-endorsed Class Life Asset Depreciation Range System (ADR) fixes reasonable useful life assumptions for all kinds of assets and spares taxpayers from justifying their replacement policies. There are three basic depreciation methods, and each has its own advantages. Your calculations should appear on Schedule C-2 (see page 2 of Schedule C in the example). Here's how they are done:

a. *The straight-line method.* Recover the property's basis, less any predicted salvage value, over its estimated useful life, in equal amounts annually. The straight-line method is ideal for young health professionals who do not want to deduct a major portion of their depreciation expenses in the first year or two of the asset's life, but would rather save most of their deductions for later years, when they expect to need them more.

b. *The declining-balance method.* Double the rate you would use in a straight-line computation and apply it against the property's cost basis that remains each year, until you're only left with a reasonable salvage value. That's the double declining-balance method, and it lets you take a big deduction the first year, terrific if you want to offset especially high current income. Double declining-balance is available only for new personal property used in a trade or business. For other assets, your declining-balance calculation is limited to 125 or 150 per cent of the straight-line rate.

c. *Sum-of-the-years' digits method.* This is the trickiest approach, but, if available for your asset, it may be the best one for you. Start by adding the digits of the number of years in your asset's useful life: if your lab equipment is supposed to last eight years, the digits 1 through 8 (1+2+3+4+5+6+7+8) total 36. Every year, deduct that part of your depreciable cost stated in the fraction:

$$\frac{years\ of\ remaining\ useful\ life}{sum\ of\ the\ year's\ digits.}$$

So, in the first year, you would deduct 8/36 of your depreciable cost.

In the second year, 7/36
In the third year, 6/36
In the fourth year, 5/36
In the fifth year, 4/36
In the sixth year, 3/36
In the seventh year, 2/36
In the eighth year, 1/36

Line 7: Total your "business" taxes, including Social Security, property, state unemployment, and, in some states, sales taxes.

Line 8: This means upkeep costs too.

Line 9: If you had *big* repairs, report them here. Incidental items can be reported under a catchall category at line 19.

Line 10: Just total the W–2s that have been prepared for your employees.

[See §§12.09 12.10] Line 11: Professional liability coverage, office liability, fire insurance on contents—all these are deductible.

Line 12: Your legal and accounting fees are obvious deductions, but did you remember the colleague who filled in for your last summer?

Line 13: This probably won't apply to you.

Line 14: Here is where you would record amortizable expenses, like leasehold improvements.

[See §2.02] Line 15: Deduct Keogh contributions made on behalf of your staff at part (a) and other fringe-benefit costs, e.g., their hospitalization insurance, at part (b).

Line 16: Interest is deductible, whether it is on your professional building's mortgage or on an equipment loan. Report interest on debts incurred to purchase investment property on Schedule A, however, not here.

Line 17: Bad debts are not deductible by a cash-basis taxpayer.

Line 18: This does not apply to you.

Line 19: All that is left to deduct goes here.

Line 20: Total everything you are deducting.

Line 21: See how the year looks.

Be careful when you deduct the expenses of a home office. You must be able to show that you use the office exclusively and regularly as your principal place of business or as a place of business where you meet or deal with patients in the normal course of your practice. In no event may deductions allocated to the use of the home office exceed the amount of gross income derived from its use.

Schedule C-1: If you do not sell goods, skip it.

Schedule C-2: We've already taken a good look at this one, but pick up on another deduction: you may be entitled to deduct a flat 20 per cent of the first $10,000 cost of depreciable property you acquired during the taxable year. This "bonus" depreciation is yours in addition to any other depreciation that's now deductible.

§5.12

SUPPORTING YOUR T. & E. WRITE-OFFS

Schedule C-3: Look out! Tax auditors have been instructed to be tougher-than-tough on travel and entertainment (T. & E.) deductions. Take a look at these recent IRS directives to its examiners and what they mean to you:

• Require the taxpayer to establish the primary purpose of the travel and the business purpose served.

Deductions aren't allowed for attendance at more than two foreign conventions in a year, and the rules of deductibility are extremely strict. Transportation cost is limited to the lowest coach fare available. If less than half the days at your convention site are business days, the deduction is limited to coach fare times business days divided by total days. Meals and lodging are capped at the per diem subsistence rate allowed federal employees in the same geographic area; and a full day's subsistence is only allowed if six hours of business activities are scheduled that day and two-thirds of them are actually attended. Only one-half day's subsistence is allowed if three hours are scheduled and two of them attended. Your only out: The limiting rules no longer apply to an employer paying the expenses of an individual attending a foreign convention, where that individual is required to include the expenses in his gross income.

To claim any other expense deduction, you must certify (as part of your return) the total days of the trip, the days and time spent traveling, the number of hours each day you devoted to scheduled business activity, and a program of the business activities. What's more, an officer of the sponsoring organization must certify (as part of your return) a schedule of business activities for each day of the convention and the number of hours each day you attended such activities.

The wise conventioneer will go further still. Hold on to seminar notes, professional literature, agendas, and so forth, and be able to prove your visit was a practice-booster and not just a pleasure jaunt.

• Be alert for possible inclusion of personal items of entertainment.

Since the examiner will be watching closely, keep a diary of the time, place, and amount you spent on T. & E. and its professional purpose. For $25-and-up items, also retain your statement of charges.

• For home parties..., determine if the benefit enjoyed by the taxpayer was of the goodwill variety derived from a purely social setting which fails to meet the "directly related" [to business] and "associated with" [business] tests [of the Internal Revenue Code].

Conservative taxpayers will save their receipts and prorate expense between professional and social guests. Parties that might have been given even without a business purpose, like weddings and birthdays, probably aren't deductible.

• For sporting events...secure all lists of the persons attending...

Maintain a who-when-and-why log to document the business relationship of your guests.

• Verify expenses directly related to an entertainment facility.

No deduction is allowed for most expenses paid for entertainment, amusement or recreational facilities. Exceptions are country club fees where use is primarily business and dues or fees paid to civic and professional organizations and business luncheon clubs.

§5.13

IT'S ALL IN HOW YOU FIGURE IT

Once you have brought your line 21 result over to line 13 of your Form 1040, you can add to it your other income to find Gross Income. "Adjust" from it, deduct what you can, and compute your Taxable Income and, with it, your tax (less any credits to which you're entitled).

Before you sign your dollars away, take a look at two tax computation breaks that just might fit your return:

[See §5.06]

1. *Income averaging.* If you're bringing home much more income this year than you did last year, don't assume your tax rate will also skyrocket. Take your average Taxable Income (plus your zero bracket amount) for the last four years and multiply that average by 120 per cent. Now you have your "base" income. Subtract that base from your current year's Taxable Income. If the difference exceeds $3,000, you are eligible for averaging. Divide that difference by 5 and add your answer to the base. Compute the tax on your income with the excess and then without it. Take the difference in those two taxes—the "excess tax"—and multiply it by 5. Then add it to the tax on the base, and you have figured your tax the "averaged" way. Schedule G makes it all look so much simpler.

The impact of averaging can be sizable. With averaging, the mythical Doctor and Mrs. Healer, who file jointly, have computed their 1978 tax liability at $12,794. Without averaging, their $50,000 income would be subject to a tax of $15,460. The tax saving amounts to $2,666, and next year they can probably average again.

If your fees dramatically jumped this taxable year, consider income averaging, but do not blindly conclude that it is for you. Your decision to average would disqualify you from applying the 50 per cent maximum tax on personal service income (see below). Review your tax liability with averaging and without it. Then decide, knowing you are right.

2. The *maximum* tax. The tax laws favor genuine productivity over "coupon-clipping." Thus, your personal service income—your professional fees, for instance—would not be taxed at a rate beyond 50 per cent. *Unearned* income, on the other hand—dividends and interest—can be taxed at all the way up to 70 per cent.

Here is how the maximum tax computation works: suppose your professional corporation pays you a salary of $203,200 and your AGI is $228,200; so, for the sake of example, is your TI. The Tax Tables would show tax of $128,480, yet Dr. Surgeon's 1978 liability is limited to $98,946. See how his tax is computed on Form 4726.

§5.14

SUCCESS!

This is the federal income tax system as it affects you today. Appreciating how it works, map out your tax tactics early. At the same time remain alert for any change in policy coming out of Washington.

SCHEDULE G
(Form 1040)
Department of the Treasury
Internal Revenue Service

Income Averaging

▶ See instructions on pages 3 and 4.
▶ Attach to Form 1040.

19--

Name(s) as shown on Form 1040	Your social security number
Cautious and Careful Healer	876 : 54 : 321

Base Period Income and Adjustments

	(a) 1st preceding base period year - - - -	(b) 2d preceding base period year - - - -	(c) 3rd preceding base period year - - - -	(d) 4th preceding base period year - - - -
1 Taxable income	22,000 00	17,000 00	12,000 00	9,000 00
2 Income earned outside of the United States or within U.S. possessions and excluded under sections 911 and 931				
3 If you checked, on {2 or 5 enter $3,200} in your - - - - Form {1 or 4 enter $2,200} each 1040, box {3 enter $1,600} column .	3,200 00	3,200 00	3,200 00	3,200 00
4 Base period income (add lines 1, 2 and 3). If less than zero, enter zero	25,200 00	20,200 00	15,200 00	12,200 00

Computation of Averageable Income

5 Taxable income for 19-- from Schedule TC (Form 1040), Part I, line 3 . . .	5	50,000 00
6 Certain amounts received by owner-employees subject to a penalty under section 72(m)(5)	6	
7 Subtract line 6 from line 5	7	50,000 00
8 Excess community income	8	
9 Adjusted taxable income (subtract line 8 from line 7). If less than zero, enter zero	9	50,000 00
10 30% of the sum of line 4, columns (a) through (d)	10	21,840 00
11 Averageable income (subtract line 10 from line 9)	11	28,160 00

Complete the remaining parts of this form only if line 11 is more than $3,000. If $3,000 or less, you do not qualify for income averaging. Do not fill in rest of form.

G

Computation of Tax

12 Amount from line 10	12	21,840 00
13 20% of line 11	13	5,632 00
14 Total (add lines 12 and 13)	14	27,472 00
15 Excess community income from line 8	15	
16 Total (add lines 14 and 15)	16	27,472 00

17 Tax on amount on line 16			17	5,758 00
18 Tax on amount on line 14	18	5,758 00		
19 Tax on amount on line 12	19	3,999 00		
20 Subtract line 19 from line 18	20	1,759 00		
21 Multiply the amount on line 20 by 4			21	7,036 00

Note: *If no entry was made on line 6 above, skip lines 22 through 24 and go to line 25.*

22 Tax on amount on line 5	22	
23 Tax on amount on line 7	23	
24 Subtract line 23 from line 22		24	
25 Tax (add lines 17, 21, and 24). Enter here and on Schedule TC (Form 1040), Part I, line 4. Also check Schedule G box on Schedule TC (Form 1040), Part I, line 4	25	12,794 00

Form **4726**
Department of the Treasury
Internal Revenue Service

Maximum Tax on Personal Service Income
▶ Attach to Form 1040 (or Form 1041).

19--

Name(s) as shown on Form 1040 (or Form 1041)	Identifying number
Successful and Satisfied Surgeon	123 - 45 - 6789

Do not complete this form if—(a) Taxable income or personal service taxable income is:

$40,200 or less, and on Form 1040, you checked box 1 or box 4,

$55,200 or less, and on Form 1040, you checked box 2 or box 5,

$26,000 or less and this is an Estate or Trust return (Form 1041);

(b) You elected income averaging; or

(c) On Form 1040, you checked box 3.

A—Personal Service Income		B—Deductions Against Personal Service Income	
Salary	203,200		
Total personal service income	203,200	Total deductions against personal service income . .	- 0 -

1 Personal service net income—Subtract total amount in column B from total amount in column A . .	1	203,200
2 Enter your adjusted gross income	2	228,200
3 Divide the amount on line 1 by the amount on line 2. Enter percentage result here, but not more than 100%	3	89.04%
4 Enter your taxable income	4	208,200
5 Multiply the amount on line 4 by the percentage on line 3	5	185,381
6 Enter the total of your 19-- tax preference items	6	-0-
7 Personal service taxable income. Subtract line 6 from line 5 (see instructions)	7	185,381
8 If: on Form 1040, you checked box 1 or box 4, enter $40,200		
on Form 1040, you checked box 2 or box 5, enter $55,200	8	55,200
Estate or Trust, enter $26,000		
9 Subtract line 8 from line 7 (if zero or less, do not complete rest of form)	9	130,181
10 Enter 50% of line 9	10	65,091
11 Tax on amount on line 4 (use Tax Rate Schedule from Form 1040 (or Form 1041) instructions)	11 114,480	
12 Tax on amount on line 7 (use Tax Rate Schedule from Form 1040 (or Form 1041) instructions)	12 98,685	
13 Subtract line 12 from line 11	13	15,795
14 If the amount on line 8 is: $40,200, enter $13,290 ($12,240 if unmarried head of household) .		
$55,200, enter $18,060	14	18,060
$26,000, enter $9,030		
15 Add lines 10, 13, and 14. This is your maximum tax. (See instructions)	15	98,946

Computation of Alternative Tax

16 Amount from line 4	16	
17 Amount from Schedule D (Form 1040), line 15(a)* (or Form 1041, page 1, line 22)	17	
18 Subtract line 17 from line 16	18	
If line 17 does not exceed $25,000, check here ▶ ☐ and omit lines 19 through 22.		
19 Enter amount from line 18 plus $25,000	19	
20 Enter amount from line 11	20	
21 Tax on amount on line 19 (use Tax Rate Schedule from Form 1040 (or 1041) instructions)	21	
22 Subtract line 21 from line 20	22	
23 Tax on amount on line 18 (use Tax Rate Schedule from Form 1040 (or 1041) instructions)	23	
24 Subtract line 23 from line 11	24	
25 Subtract line 24 from line 15	25	
26 If the block on line 18 is checked, enter 50% of line 17; otherwise, enter $12,500	26	
27 Alternative tax, add lines 22 (if applicable), 25 and 26. (See instructions)	27	

* If you reported capital gain distributions but did not use Schedule D (Form 1040), enter on line 17 the amount shown on Form 1040, line 15.

235–166—1

Form **4726** (19--)

CHAPTER **6**

MULTIPLYING
YOUR DOLLARS

§6.01

YOUR LAWYER'S ROLE

One self-acclaimed "indispensable" book after another preaches *the* sure-fire way to invest: when you should invest, how much, and even which investment is right for you. Unfortunately, the answers are just not that cut-and-dried. Investing in anything is taking a risk, and nobody can honestly tell you with certainty that investment A is absolutely better for you than investment B. The ultimate decision must remain yours—and so will the profit or the loss. Once you put your money on the line, you are on your own. But first, ask your lawyer for some help in your investment planning:

1. Learn your attorney's candid opinion about your financial preparedness for investing. Your lawyer will review your current income and your current expenses, and will project the growth of your practice and realistically predict how much additional capital you might eventually need to realize your professional goals. Your lawyer can also guess how much money your family might require for your children's education, significant medical bills, or other major expenses. He will be able to quote rules of thumb about how much cash you should always keep on hand for emergencies, and determine whether or not you have adequate insurance protection. Only then can you see what, if anything, is left for investing.
2. Once it is known how much you can afford to invest, your lawyer can assist you in defining your investment objectives. Should you be looking for steady income, capital appreciation, or some happy medium? Are you able to speculate, or should you stick to conservative investments? Would you be wise to diversify your holdings, or would you be better off keeping your money in one place, where you can closely watch your investment's progress?
3. Now you are agreed on philosophy. The big issue remains, "Exactly which investments fit my requirements and my goals?" Your lawyer cannot answer that question for you but can give you some pretty informative advice, advice worth seeking before you invest.

At the base of any investment is a contract: you are paying your dollars in return for X, Y, or Z. You might be getting an ownership interest in a major corporation, one that has enjoyed tremendous profits in recent years; or you might be buying a parcel of land in Florida, where a retirement village will soon be booming; or you might be giving a governmental unit a loan in exchange for a promise of repayment along with interest.

Whatever the vehicle, there will be all kinds of external influences acting upon your investment, increasing or decreasing its chances for success. But you will want to know all you can before you invest. Learn what your contractual rights would be—and, for that matter, your contractual obligations, too. You will also want to know that the structure of the investment is legally sound. Beyond these, you will be concerned about any personal tax advantages—or disadvantages—you would buy, were you to invest.

That's where your attorney comes in. A lawyer can see if an "opportunity" is really an opportunity from a legal vantage point. Is it well-conceived? Are there adequate controls? In addition, apart from its intrinsic merit, does it make sense for you in particular?

We ought to examine a few of the more popular ways of investing, and note some of the pluses and minuses your lawyer might find.

§6.02

HOW STOCK CAN MAKE YOU MONEY

Let's start with stock. There are two kinds: *common* and *preferred*. Common stockholders are owners of corporations, thereby entitled to a proportionate share of distributed profits, or *dividends*. They become decision-makers in that they can annually vote for corporate directors. What's more, they have the right to help decide very major "organic" questions which might confront their corporations. In reality, however, investors play a passive role. After all, they are interested in money-making, not policy-making, and they are content to see their votes count no more than those of the thousands of other common stockholders who own the corporations.

When a corporation originally sells its common stock to the public, the stock's price is fixed. Thereafter, the laws of supply and demand govern. As the company prospers, the common stockholder's shares become more valuable on the marketplace. Especially with uncertain market conditions, common stock is sometimes a volatile investment, and dividends are often unpredictable. Happily the potential for growth many times is realized, and that, of course, makes the risks all worthwhile.

Preferred stock, in contrast, is a stable investment. Its essence is its dividend return. While common stock dividends are discretionary with the directors and conditioned upon adequate company earnings, preferred stock dividends are fixed in advance, so preferred stock price fluctuations are minimal. The preferred stockholder is more a financial backer, with a well-protected investment, than a company owner. No common stock dividends are payable until all dividend obligations to preferred stockholders are met. What's more, should the corporation dissolve, net company assets are distributable to preferred stockholders first, and then to common stockholders. Typically, the preferred stockholder cannot participate in management decisions but enjoys investment security second only to a bondholder.

§6.03

ARE MUTUAL FUNDS THE ANSWER?

You will often hear that diversifying your stock portfolio might be wise if you are investing a *large* sum of money; only then can you really spread your risk without dissipating your effort. So it *was*. Today, however, with the popularity of mutual funds, the average investor can diversify without regard to the size of his or her portfolio. One can buy mutual fund shares and inexpensively gain the benefit of professional investment management. Some mutual funds have performed excellently, yet as in any direct stock investment, uncertainties remain. A few commonsense pointers will lead you to "the right fund" for you.

1. Know yourself. How much do you have to invest? What are your other investments? How old are you? How well can you sleep at night when you really speculate? In short, you have got to sit down and sincerely determine what you are after.
2. When looking at funds, discount the importance of their long-term records. As impressive as they may be, you are only interested in what the fund's present management can do with a fund its present size, so look at last year.
3. Satisfy yourself that success was not just good luck. If management plotted a sound course and followed it, that's great. You will know what plans management had, if any, from the Annual Report of the year before. If management was as surprised at its success as you were to learn of it, move on to another fund.
4. Find out which stocks were held and why. If there seems to be a pattern of logic to each purchase and sale, that is an advantage. Don't lose confidence if management was wrong, however. Thoughtful planning is what you are buying, not guaranteed results.
5. Match goals. Funds primarily invest in U.S. common stocks, but they can also buy preferred stocks, bonds, and Canadian securities, and in any combination. Some are "blue chip" and others are highly speculative. Some specialize and invest in oil, chemicals, or steel alone. For your own satisfaction, relate your personal needs to the goals of the fund and make sure they match. Among the most significant considerations to be checked out are safety, income, growth, and flexibility.
6. Consider a new fund. It won't be carrying stagnant securities thought to be "comers" years ago.
7. Do not downgrade the small fund. Big funds can be unwieldy. Moreover, if a few million of their dollars are brilliantly invested, the results might not even show at the shareholder level.
8. Give some thought to diversifying among funds. If mutual funds are a good idea, diversifying among them can be an even better one for some investors.
9. Once you buy into a fund, get out if it does not perform. Do not hold your fund to a lower standard than you would hold any other investment.

§6.04

EVALUATING AN ON-GOING CONCERN AS AN INVESTMENT RISK

Stock is an exciting investment. In fact, one out of every six Americans is seeking his fortune by riding the coattails of Big and Not-So-Big Business. Before you let yourself be swept away by glamor, get a copy of the company's Annual Report to Shareholders. Your lawyer will want to review the concern's *Balance Sheet* or *Statement of Condition,* its *Income Statement,* and its *Statement of Owners' Equity.* Read together, they will define the corporation's financial strengths and weaknesses in objective terms.

A *Balance Sheet* spells out the condition of a company as of a certain date. The classical account form itemizes assets on the left side of the page, liabilities and capital on the right. As accountants would say, the debits to the left must equal the credits to the right. The specimen report form that follows sets out the "right-hand" items directly below the "left-hand" items, graphically emphasizing the fact that any shareholders' rights fall below the earlier claims of outside creditors.

THE THIGAMAJIG CORPORATION
Position Statement

August 1, 1978

Thousands of Dollars

Assets

Current Assets
Cash	$10,000	
Accounts receivable	10,000	
Merchandise inventory	20,000	
Prepaid rent and insurance	5,000	$45,000

Fixed Assets
Building and land	$10,000	
Furniture, fixtures, and equipment	5,000	$15,000
		$60,000

Liabilities and Capital

Current Liabilities
Accounts payable	$ 5,000	
Notes payable	13,000	
Dividends payable	5,000	$23,000

Deferred Liabilities
Accrued federal and state income taxes	$ 2,000	
Accumulated deferred income taxes	10,000	
Accumulated deferred investment tax credit	5,000	$17,000

Capitalization
Common stock—no par value, 2,000,000 shares at	$10,000	
Retained earnings	5,000	
LESS: Capital stock expense	750	$14,250
Preferred stock	$ 3,000	
Long-term debt	2,750	5,750
		$20,000
		$60,000

An *Income Statement* is commonly called a *Profit and Loss Statement* (P & L). It lists the various kinds of income that were received during an accounting period and the amount of each kind, the expenses incurred in earning that income, and the difference, *net profit*. Income statements often look like this one:

WONDER WIDGET COMPANY
Income Statement

From April 1, 1978, to June 30, 1978

Net Sales		$1,000,000
LESS: Cost of goods sold		600,000
		$ 400,000
Expenses		
Selling expenses	$ 50,000	
General and administrative expense	100,000	
Financial expense	15,000	
Total expenses		165,000
Net operating profit		235,000
PLUS: nonoperating income		5,000
Net profit		$ 240,000

We have seen that a Balance Sheet is a listing of corporate assets and liabilities, as of one minute frozen in time. A P & L shows where income came from and what was paid out from it before stockholders saw net earnings.

The *Statement of Owners' Equity* is the puzzle's final piece, the one that completes the picture. This report states what rights shareholders had at the beginning and at the end of an accounting period and how the difference can be explained. Here is how a Statement of Owners' Equity might look:

HOOTENHOLLAR CORPORATION
Statement of Owners' Equity

From April 1, 1978, to June 30, 1978

Retained Earnings, April 1			$10,000
PLUS:			
Net operating profit for the quarter	$10,000		
Net profit from investments	2,000	12,000	$22,000
LESS:			
Dividends declared		5,000	
Retained earnings capitalized as common stock		5,000	10,000
			$12,000
Retained Earnings, June 30			

When you study any financial report, bear these thoughts in mind:

1. It is dated. Make sure you are looking at the most recent statement available. Even a few days can bring a dramatic change.
2. Jargon abounds, but do not let the terminology intimidate you. Current assets are liquid assets. Fixed assets are nothing more than property, plant, and equipment. Current liabilities are short-term debts. Fixed liabilities are long-term debts. Your lawyer will be glad to define the other terms you will need to understand.
3. Painful truths are often buried in footnotes and parenthetical comments. Keep an eye out for contingent obligations, for instance.
4. If a report refers you to an elaborating schedule, by all means interpret that additional data. Of selling expenses, how much is being written off as bad debts? Of administrative expenses, what portion goes to executive salaries? Where does that nonoperating income come from?
5. When possible, compare the report you have been given with earlier reports. Comparative analysis can help you appreciate corporate trends, crucial in the projection of future prospects.

In reviewing financial statements, you or your lawyer might relate one accounting element to another. Although a purely mathematical evaluation leads to a simplistic conclusion, *ratio analysis* can be very helpful in scrutinizing a company's operation. Check these relationships, for instance:

1. *Sales trend.* If a company enjoyed gross sales of $300,000 last year but sales of only $200,000 the year before, we are talking about a 3:2 ratio. In most industries, a continuation of that trend, or anything like it, over even a few years would presage good things to come.
2. *Working capital.* This is the amount of money a firm needs to meet its very immediate liabilities and any exigencies. Subtract current liabilities from current assets, and working capital is what you have left. If current assets are $1,000,000 and current liabilities are $750,000, working capital is $250,000. Expressed as a ratio, working capital becomes $1,000,000 to $750,000 or 4:3. Conservative counselors usually hope to find a 2:1 ratio.

3. *Net income to net worth.* The rate of return being earned by owners' equity is critically important. If owners' equity is $1,000,000 and it produces $100,000 in income, the company can boast a 10:1 ratio and a 10 per cent return on its shareholders' investment dollars.

4. *Net income to net sales.* Contrast this company's net income–to–net sales ratio with others in the industry. You will be comparing the profitability of the concern you might be backing with that of its competition.

Even after all available financial statements are dissected, your lawyer probably won't be ready to advise you. These are some additional factors to be considered:

1. The quality of management
2. Market prospects
3. Any merger plans
4. Chances for entering into any new contracts and their presumed effect
5. Patent and copyright ownership

§6.05

HOW TO EVALUATE A NEW PUBLICLY HELD COMPANY

Suppose the corporation that interests you is only now going public. It's got no track record, or a limited one, probably no management susceptible to easy evaluation, no financial data that are very informative. How do you investigate the risk? Before any public stock offering, a company must issue a *Preliminary Prospectus*, the so-called "Red Herring." The printing of a Preliminary Prospectus by no means implies that a stock issue will even be floated. The Prospectus simply serves as notice that a registration statement has been filed with the Securities and Exchange Commission. SEC approval should not be taken for granted, and if stock does become available to you, you can learn a great deal about the offering by thoroughly digesting the Red Herring. Check these risk factors against any Preliminary Prospectus that crosses your desk:

1. Is the asking price per share too high? Any new issue has as its primary risk the absence of a market for its shares. Price must be arbitrarily determined, but does it seem realistic in light of the company's apparent potential and the number of shares being offered?
2. Is this a brand-new enterprise? If so, the firm has no established credit, no goodwill, and certainly no customers. It may be a year or more, in fact, until any sales income can be anticipated.
3. Might the company need additional financing in the near future? If so, and if that financing cannot easily be found, operations might be hampered.
4. Are manufacturing facilities yet to be constructed or located and purchased? There may be a problem in finding an appropriate site at the right price. Moreover, mortgage financing might be difficult to obtain on favorable terms.
5. Does a competitor have the edge? It is likely that other companies have more money and more technical expertise. If technological development is the crux of this firm's future, recognize its limitations.
6. How much governmental regulation affects the firm's activities? Existing or proposed legislation might make the operation more costly to run, thus less profitable.
7. Does the firm hold any patents? If not, what does it intend to do that others cannot do better?

8. How dependent is the firm on a few people? All companies are tremendously dependent on their important employees, but could this firm overcome the death or resignation of one or more of its officers?
9. How will your interest be diluted as additional shares are issued? In this regard, you will want to know what stock options have been granted to key personnel.
10. Does the proposed use of proceeds make sense?
11. Is the capital structure sound? What rights does each class of stock bear?
12. What property does the firm own?
13. Who is the management?
14. What compensation is to be paid to the various officers?
15. What transactions have taken place between the company and the management as private individuals?
16. Who are the principal stockholders?

§6.06

IS THERE A WAY TO WIN?

Traditionally, making money in the stock market only results from buying low and selling high. Your lawyer can tell you if the company you are looking at seems to be solvent and well-structured, and your broker can tell you about market conditions and industry prospects. Most of the other unknowns can only be guessed at. Therein lies the risk of making it big or losing it fast. A couple of investment techniques can minimize your downward risk:

1. One is *dollar cost averaging.* Decide how much you want to invest every month, every two months, or every six months and buy as much of the one stock you have selected as those dollars will buy. You cannot waiver from your purchase schedule no matter which direction your stock's price is traveling. At times, some might say you are fighting a lost cause, but statistically, at least, you ought to emerge a victor. The secret's pretty obvious: you will be buying more shares when the price is low than when it is high. You are committed to a periodic fixed dollar investment. Consequently, when your stock rises—or, more accurately, if your stock rises—you will realize a profit on all the shares you bought at a cheaper price, offset only by the loss on those relatively few shares you bought at a premium.
2. Another investment technique worth mentioning is *formula investing.* The "formula" dictates how your investment portfolio will be split between stock and bonds. Once stock prices soar, it is a good time to sell your stock and buy bonds. When the stock market drops, take advantage of the lower prices and trade your bonds in for stock; with luck, they will rebound. In practice, the theory works but proves far from perfect; the few stocks you own are not guaranteed to perform as well or as poorly as the market on the whole. Even so, formula investing remains a prudent tool worth considering in your investment planning. Formula advocates design their investment programs in one of three ways:
   (a) *Constant-dollar plans.* The idea is to keep a predetermined dollar amount in the stock market no matter what happens. Suppose you decide to invest $25,000 and, in a year, your stock appreciates 10 per cent. Now your portfolio is worth $27,500. You want to maintain $25,000 in stock—no more, no less. Thus, your constant-dollar approach will require you to take your $2,500 profit and buy bonds with it. Should the value of your stock drop below $25,000, you would sell bonds to make up the difference. Through a

constant-dollar plan, you might achieve some success in balanced investing, but if stock steadily climbs in value, your fixed dollar commitment will foreclose some stock investment opportunities.

(b) *Constant-ratio plans.* Here you can take advantage of the anticipated upward movement in stock prices over the long term. Instead of restricting the *amount* of your investment in the stock market, restrict the *percentage.* Split your portfolio right down the middle and maintain half your funds in stock, half in bonds. If the stock depreciates in value, sell some bonds and buy more stock. If the stock appreciates, sell some. Just keep your investment dollars appropriately divided between stock and bonds.

(c) *Variable-ratio plans.* The goal of this plan is to make the most of long-term market cycles as well as short-term fluctuations. Balance your investment in stock and bonds, perhaps half your investment dollars in each at first. Then, when conditions look right, change the ratio. When the stock market jumps X per cent, reduce the fraction of your portfolio devoted to stock. If only the stock and bond markets could really be beaten by a slide rule!

One point ought to be remembered. When stocks reach a new high, that is the time to look at bonds—despite the inevitable optimism on Wall Street.

§6.07

WHAT'S A BOND?

A *bond* is nothing more than the promise of a government or a corporation to repay the money you loan it at a certain time and with interest. What is behind that promise? Sometimes property is mortgaged, and then you've got a secured investment. Other times, you may be relying on the issuer's general assets and good name, much like an individual's signature loan. Either way, invest in high-grade bonds, and you can count on punctual repayment and steady interest income. What you won't get is growth, but you may not mind that shortcoming.

§6.08

TAX-EXEMPT MUNICIPALS

The tax advantages to be gained from *municipal bonds,* for instance, many times offset the lack of growth potential. When a state or city needs to raise money for community improvements, it will issue bonds to realize revenue. You can expect only a small interest rate, but the income you will receive will be federal income tax–free. For investors in the upper brackets, that effectively means more net profit. For example, if you are in the 45 per cent tax bracket and purchase a 7 per cent *nonexempt* bond, your after-tax income is 3.85 per cent. With a good municipal, you can probably earn 5 per cent or more, net.

The following chart helps show what tax-exempt income might mean to you. Find your taxable income (after deductions and exemptions) and learn what taxable rate of return you'd need to earn to achieve a 5, 5 1/2, and 6 per cent tax-exempt yield.

TAXABLE INCOME		TAX BRACKET (%)	A TAX EXEMPT YIELD OF		
			5%	5-1/2%	6%
Joint Return	Single Return		IS EQUIVALENT TO A TAXABLE YIELD OF:		
$ 20,200- 24,600		28	6.94%	7.64%	8.33%
	$ 15,000- 18,200	30	7.14	7.86	8.57
$ 24,600- 29,900		32	7.35	8.09	8.82
	$ 18,200- 23,500	34	7.58	8.33	9.09
$ 29,900- 35,200		37	7.94	8.73	9.52
	$ 23,500- 28,800	39	8.20	9.02	9.84
$ 35,200- 45,800		43	8.77	9.65	10.52
	$ 28,800- 34,100	44	8.93	9.82	10.71
$ 45,800- 60,000	$ 34,100- 41,500	49	9.80	10.78	11.76
$ 60,000- 85,600		54	10.87	11.96	13.04
	$ 41,500- 55,300	55	11.11	12.22	13.33
$ 85,600-109,400		59	12.20	13.41	14.63
	$ 55,300- 81,800	63	13.51	14.86	16.21
$109,400-162,400		64	13.89	15.28	16.66
$162,400-215,400	$ 81,800-108,300	68	15.63	17.18	18.75
$215,400 & over	$108,300 & over	70	16.67	18.33	20.00

The advantage mutual funds offer in diversification has already been discussed. Now that bonus can be yours through investment in a tax-exempt bond fund. What's more, earnings can compound tax-free, sweetening your yield beyond expectations. For example:

1. If a 5 1/2 per cent dividend were paid out on a $10,000 investment over a term of ten years, the *simple dividend return* would be $550 each year.

Year 1	Year 2	Year 3	Year 4	Year 5	Year 6	Year 7	Year 8	Year 9	Year 10
$550	$1,100	$1,650	$2,200	$2,750	$3,300	$3,850	$4,400	$4,950	$5,500

2. Your *simple rate of return* would remain stable.

Year 1	Year 2	Year 3	Year 4	Year 5	Year 6	Year 7	Year 8	Year 9	Year 10
5.5%	5.5%	5.5%	5.5%	5.5%	5.5%	5.5%	5.5%	5.5%	5.5%

3. If you were in the 40 per cent tax bracket, you'd pay $367 in tax on a taxable $10,000 investment returning 9.17 per cent. Your net retained return would remain constant at $5.50 or 5.5 per cent, and your *taxable equivalent rate of return* would remain stable.

Year 1	Year 2	Year 3	Year 4	Year 5	Year 6	Year 7	Year 8	Year 9	Year 10
9.17%	9.17%	9.17%	9.17%	9.17%	9.17%	9.17%	9.17%	9.17%	9.17%

4. Now reinvest dividends in additional dividend-paying shares, and marvel at the miracle of compounding. Look at your *compound dividend return*, the total of all dividends paid during the course of the year.

Year 1	Year 2	Year 3	Year 4	Year 5	Year 6	Year 7	Year 8	Year 9	Year 10
$550	$1,130	$1,742	$2,388	$3,070	$3,788	$4,547	$5,347	$6,191	$7,081

5. Look also at the *equivalent average simple rate of return,* the rate you'd have to earn to receive cash dividends equal to your compound dividend return. When the $550 you earn in year 1 is reinvested, a 5 1/2 per cent simple rate of return on the new base of $10,554 in year 2 generates $580 in dividends. The total return of $1,130 over two years is equivalent to an average simple rate of return of 5.65 per cent for each year (5.650% × $10,000 = $565 × 2 = $1,130).

Year 1	Year 2	Year 3	Year 4	Year 5	Year 6	Year 7	Year 8	Year 9	Year 10
5.50%	5.650%	5.807%	5.970%	6.140%	6.313%	6.495%	6.684%	6.879%	7.081%

6. Again if one assumes a 40 per cent bracket, the *taxable equivalent average simple rate of return* is astounding.

Year 1	Year 2	Year 3	Year 4	Year 5	Year 6	Year 7	Year 8	Year 9	Year 10
9.17%	9.42%	9.68%	9.95%	10.23%	10.52%	10.83%	11.14%	11.47%	11.80%

§6.09

MORE ON BONDS AND INCOME

Taxable or tax-exempt, your interest will be paid to you automatically if your bond is issued in *registered form*—that is, if your name and address appear on the instrument. Otherwise, the bond is issued in *bearer form*. Since the issuer presumably does not know the bond is yours, you have to clip a coupon periodically and send it in to receive your payment.

How great a return you will enjoy has a lot to do with supply-and-demand factors in the bond market and interest rates generally. Bonds are issued in $1,000 denominations and are usually traded over-the-counter. The stated interest rate will reflect the track record of the individual issuer and, as we have seen, the level of the stock market.

Once a bond has been issued, its stated rate of interest has less influence on the return subsequent purchasers will realize than you might think. Along with investor enthusiasm and interest-rate shifts, bond prices fluctuate continually. Of course, the lower the price of the bond, the greater return a stated interest percentage represents.

Suppose you buy a $1,000 bond at $500. (Your price would be quoted as 50, meaning 50 per cent of face value.) If stated interest is 4 per cent, you will earn 4 per cent of the $1,000 face value or $40, which represents an 8 per cent return on the $500 investment. On the other hand, buying a bond *above* face value will reduce your rate of return.

More often than not, good quality bonds offer conservative investors a safe and steady return on their capital, without the anxiety or the excitement of substantial appreciation. The following debt instruments are very popular today:

1. *Treasury bills.* These are obligations of the U.S. government. T-bills, recently yielding 6.8 per cent, require a minimum investment of $10,000 and are available in original maturities of three months to one year. Interest is exempt from state and local income taxes.

2. *Treasury notes.* In $1,000 denominations, these mature in one to seven years and recently paid between 7 and 7 1/2 per cent. The term dictates the yield. These, too, are exempt from state and local taxes.

3. *Treasury bonds.* Again available in $1,000 denominations, original maturities are five years or less. The yield is about the same as you'd find in T-notes, and, again, state and local taxes don't apply.

4. *U.S. agency short-term notes.* These are issued by federal agencies or agencies under federal sponsorship and sold by commercial banks or brokers. The minimum investment is $5,000. The yield you might expect is 6 3/4 per cent or better, usually free of state and local income tax.

5. *Project notes.* Issued by local housing agencies and sold by banks or brokers, these instruments are also backed by the U.S. government. Highly liquid and very safe, project notes provide interest that is exempt from tax by the federal government and the issuer's state; that's why the yield is only about 3 1/2 per cent.

6. *Commercial paper.* This is short-term debt, issued on a discount basis by major corporations, with or without bank backing. The minimum investment is $25,000; 6 1/2 per cent is the recent yield. Only consider top-rated (A-1 or Prime-1) paper.

7. *Convertible corporate bonds.* Present interest rates are good, and you have the right to "convert" into common stock and enjoy capital appreciation.

§6.10

WHO ARE GINNIE MAE AND FREDDY MAC?

Much like bonds, and in some ways even better, are *Ginnie Mae's*—Government National Mortgage Association (GNMA) securities. These are blanket home mortgages with interest running about 8 1/2 per cent, ever-increasing returns of principal, and prepayments. Ginnie Mae supplements the secondary mortgage market by making residential mortgage investments more liquid. It can do quite a bit for your investment package, too.

If you invest $25,000, the minimum Ginnie Mae investment, you can expect about $350 back each month. That represents interest, repaid principal, and prepayment. Yet only interest income is taxable. (Every month, interest decreases and principal increases.) Even capital gains can be yours through Ginnie Mae's if you purchase them below par and then interest rates drop. Best of all, Ginnie Mae is guaranteed by the quasi-governmental agency that runs the program *and* the Federal Housing Administration or the Veterans' Administration. You will receive your full payment each month even if the underlying mortgage is foreclosed.

If Ginnie Mae is too rich for your blood, consider *Freddy Mac.* The Federal National Mortgage Association buys mortgages from originating banks and savings associations, pools them, adds its own guarantee, and sells participating interests to long-term investors. Units are $10,000 each, and the yield is now about 8 per cent compared with Ginnie Mae's 8 1/2 per cent.

§6.11

A FINAL WORD

Whatever investment vehicle you elect, remember you are dealing in a very sophisticated medium. Arm yourself with knowledgeable and talented counselors, and good luck!

CHAPTER 7

TAX SHELTERS:
Reaping What You Sow
and Then Some

§7.01

THE SPECIAL VIRTUES OF SHELTERS

Once upon a time, talk was about oil depletion allowance, accelerated depreciation, tax-free cash flow, and big, big cash returns. To the casual investor, tax shelters brought to mind a whole range of sophisticated, little understood Revenue Code loopholes and other assorted gimmicks thought to be employed by sharp money managers in their creation of windfall profits.

The concept, as conservative lawyers would discuss it, was far less glamorous. In fact, it all comes down to understanding the tax laws and using them to effect tax reductions. The government wants you to put your money into certain kinds of projects, projects that aid national productivity, for instance. Therefore, Congress will give you a tax break as an incentive. Putting your spare dollars into Project A rather than Project B may mean tax-free cash in your pocket.

Today, an investor doesn't look to highly leveraged timber royalties, master recordings, book manuscripts, and patents as devices for offsetting current income. Deductions are usually limited to the amount "at risk" in an investment, and front-end deductions for many kinds of prepayments are also severely limited.

Still, tax shelters do remain. Many are less exotic than they once were. Many make economic sense, even without regard to tax write-offs. Moreover, if you're a suitable investor, the best of them may be far more relevant to your own investment planning than yesterday's cattle breeding and citrus groves ever were.

The best tax shelters will do three things for you:

- They will let you deduct most of your initial investment in computing your next income tax obligation.
- During the holding period, whatever income your investment reaps will grow tax-free.
- At the end of your investment, you will get back all you invested at a lower-than-usual tax rate—or you will get back much more than you invested, taxed at the usual rate or even a higher one.

[See Chapters 2 and 4]

We have seen the concept at work in Keogh and IRA Plans and in Corporate Retirement Plans. Convert today's tax deductions into gains which will be taxed at low

46

rates later and accumulate the income on your investments tax-free, all because you have decided to invest in a congressionally favored project—employee retirement security.

§7.02

ARE YOU A SHELTER CANDIDATE?

Before looking at other shelters, we ought to check your eligibility. Tax shelters are not for everyone. Their successful use demands that you be of a temperament to live with them, and that your assets and earnings justify participation. In order to be a "sheltered" investor, you should meet the following requirements:

1. You really ought to be in the 50 per cent tax bracket or a higher one. Sheltered investments usually pose high risks, risks that are not warranted for investors in lower brackets.
2. A good candidate for tax shelters probably has substantial liquid assets, along with a healthy cash reserve for emergencies. More and more investors, however, are borrowing their investment funds. The decision to borrow should only be made if you realistically expect your investment program to be a resounding success, easily justifying your interest expense. Ideally, the resulting tax savings can then help repay your loan.
3. Once you sink a significant portion of your savings into a relatively risky venture, you are bound to fear for the safety of those dollars. It is human nature. You will know that you leaped with both eyes wide open, after learning all there was to learn about the project and its chances of success. You will remember, too, that your lawyer and your accountant reviewed your investment program and, within the limits of their professional judgment, gave it their blessings. Sit back, try to relax, and let your investment work for you. That may be the hardest part of investing, but it is crucial. If you do not think you will comfortably be able to rely on your own business acumen and the technical expertise of investment counselors, sheltered investing is just not for you. Dollar considerations aside, tax shelters are only recommended for the investor who is not overburdened by the emotional stress of risk-taking.

§7.03

THE REAL ESTATE BOOM

If you are financially and psychologically ready for a sheltered investment, chances are you have considered real estate. No doubt, investors you know are realizing good cash returns—which may run to 12 per cent and even beyond—as well as tax benefits from real estate syndication. All the while, in the face of devastating inflation, their property seems to be consistently appreciating in value. In spite of sweeping changes in our tax laws, real estate remains a deservedly popular shelter:

- A large share of the dollars you invest probably will be borrowed. Since real estate investments are thus "leveraged" investments, the return on your cash outlay will be great—if the project proves successful, of course. Within limits, the interest you pay the lender is tax-deductible, too. [See §5.01]
- Current expenses, commitment fees, standby fees—all these as well may be fully deductible during the first year. All in all, you might be able to deduct *more* than your cash contribution and, since real estate investments aren't subject to the "at risk" limitation, use your net tax loss to offset taxable income you have received from other sources during the year.

[See §5.01] • While land itself is said never to depreciate in value, buildings surely do. You can therefore deduct your cost over a building's "useful life." Just how long that "useful life" is varies from time to time and place to place. Right now, for example, most new apartment buildings in Illinois are projected to be "useful" for 33 to 35 years, while in California depreciation deductions are calculable for a 25- to 30-year term. The shorter a building's expected "useful life," the more you can deduct for depreciation each year of that life.

Some real estate investments are eligible for *accelerated* depreciation, in which greater deductions can be taken in the early years of the project's term. That way, depreciation can act as a deduction for tax purposes without being an actual cash expenditure. You can increase your initial tax loss and make more of your tax shelter.

Let us contrast the standard straight-line depreciation with an accelerated method. Suppose your syndicate invests $100,000 in real estate projected to have a useful life of 30 years. The straight-line computation would allow the group to deduct 1/30 of the total investment each year, or $3,333.33. If your syndicate were the "first user" of a new apartment building, however, you would be able to take advantage of the so-called "150 per cent declining balance" method. Your first-year deduction would become $4999.99, 1-1/2 times the straight-line deduction. Add that deduction to all your initial expenses, including deductible interest on whatever part of your $100,000 was borrowed, and you will probably find that your investment partnership's deductible outflow exceeds its cash income. Of course, you are personally entitled to your share of the partnership losses.

One word of caution: when you sell your property, the depreciation you have deducted beyond that allowed by the straight-line computation might be "recaptured"—that is, taxed as ordinary income. When your property is sold, presumably at a gain, much of your profit will be taxable at low capital gains rates.

[See §5.04] A real estate tax shelter is merely a timing device. Its first-year tax results will invariably be impressive. Heavy deductions will become immediately available to you. But what happens after that first year? Early tax savings are ordinarily matched and sometimes outweighed by later tax costs. The whole project, right up to the liquidation date, must be analyzed by a prospective investor. Moreover, the glamor of immediate tax reductions cannot overshadow the basic issue: is this project really a good business risk?

§7.04

CHECKING OUT A LIMITED PARTNERSHIP

Most real estate syndicates are structured as limited partnerships with one or more managing general partners who remain personally liable for the debts of the enterprise, and passive limited partners whose only liability is their contribution. Before you become a limited partner, your lawyer will want to check these points:

1. *The project's feasibility.* Is the land zoned to permit the construction of the kind of building that's proposed? Are there any defects in title? Might the building's construction or maintenance be violative of pollution laws? Is adequate construction financing and permanent financing available, and at what terms? You will want your initial investment refunded if any of these problems becomes insurmountable.

    How much will the land cost, and is that price reasonable? Once a building is built, will it be rentable or marketable? Who will manage it?

2. *The limited partnership's operation.* Is there really a limited partnership? Has a Certificate of Limited Partnership been executed and recorded in compliance with state law? Will the entity be empowered to assess you beyond your intended contribution? It just may be that your liability would exceed the investment commitment you are prepared to make.

Who will make decisions? You will want to restrict the authority of limited partners, or else you may be deemed a general partner, with unlimited personal liability. You will want to be consulted, however, and have some say on big questions, like the sale of major partnership assets. In addition, you will want effective control over the real decision-makers, the general partners. For one thing, insist on certified audits at least annually. For another, your partnership agreement ought to specify grounds for the removal of a general partner: death, insolvency, malfeasance, and any others that seem appropriate.

[See §1.02]

3. *Protecting your investment.* In the event the partnership is not formed, your initial contribution should be guaranteed refundable, immediately and with interest. Your funds ought to be held in a special, untouchable escrow account until the Certificate of Limited Partnership is recorded and enough money is raised to assure construction.

Carefully note the partnership's proposed capitalization. You will certainly want enough cash in the project to pay deductible expenses and maximize your shelter.

[See §6.04]

What if the partnerships runs out of money before rent-up? Can the general partners contribute more funds, and will they? If so, will they merely advance loans, and on what terms?

4. *Cash flow.* What is your anticipated cash return, and how will it be shared with the general partners? First, how is "return" defined, as cash or cash and tax benefits? What about appreciation: how is that shared? Finally, how will you share in the proceeds when the property is ultimately sold? Is your cash flow going to be guaranteed by the general partners? If so, for how long—for a set term, until you have received a prescribed yield, until the building has achieved a certain rental rate, or when? Most important, what assets are behind the guarantee?

5. *The promoter.* The stature and ability of the promoter, above all else, will determine the success or failure of a real estate investment. This individual will have the greatest responsibility for making the project happen. The ultimate question, upon which the decision to invest or not often rests, is simply, who is the promoter? What is this person's track record? Has it been characterized by honesty and trustworthiness? Have able legal and accounting counsel been retained? If the promoter is a general partner, what are his or her financial assets? Will conflicts of interest be a problem?

§7.05

THE PROMOTER'S JOB

The promoter's profit is often thought to be out of proportion to his or her cash investment. Remember, though, promoters are not contracted for their money, but rather for their skill, talent, and labor. The very sources of their remuneration prove in how many ways they are vital to a project's success:

1. First, the promoter is the syndicator, many times earning a mark-up on the package itself.
2. The promoter may be eligible for brokerage commissions when the land is bought by the syndicate and, much later, when it sells it.

3. The promoter might earn a commission when you are sold your participating interest.
4. Fees for managing the syndicate and more for managing the real estate may well be the promoter's as may bonuses on a per-rental basis.
5. The promoter may be eligible for still more fees when financing is arranged.
6. Commissions for obtaining insurance coverage on the property might be paid to the promoter, if he or she is an insurance broker.
7. In the end, the promoter may share your profits with you.

All these payments may be richly deserved. They are incentive in nature and should not be offensive to you if they are embodied in your partnership agreement. In fact, they may well work to your benefit. But carefully watch the timing of payments to promoters. Most of their compensation should be predicated on the overall success of the project, and most of their profit should be realized after success is achieved. It is only fair that they should share the element of risk with you, especially since they alone can minimize most risks as the project develops.

Given a feasible project, a highly qualified promoter, a substantial general partner, well-insulated personal involvement on your part, and a little luck, your investment in real estate can offer you a high yield, an enviable tax shelter, and even some appreciation in value. Yet, even under these seemingly ideal circumstances, you will have committed yourself to a long-term, illiquid investment.

No shelter is perfect. None is automatically profitable or even very predictable. Most are relatively high in risk and require heavy reliance on their promoters. They all demand your homework: the pivotal business decision to invest or not to invest will remain yours alone, so gather all the facts you can and review them with your lawyer and accountant.

§7.06

SHELTERS BEYOND YOUR BACKYARD

Any shelter invitation deserves the same level of scrutiny as we have suggested in the real estate context. Retain that thought when considering these sheltered opportunities:

1. *Equipment leasing.* Under the typical net lease, equipment is leased for a term approximating its useful life. The lessee assumes property taxes and insurance costs. Lease payments enable the investor-lessor to service the debt he incurred to purchase the property, to pay other expenses, and to create a small positive cash flow, so his risk is at a minimum. Tax shelter benefits arise through losses created by accelerated depreciation deductions and ordinary interest payments during the lease's early years. Here the investor's tax liability is deferred to future years; in the meantime, he is the recipient of an interest-free government loan of his or her tax dollars.
2. *Annuities.* The deferred annuity temporarily appears to be outside the clutches of the Ways and Means Committee. Stockbrokers sell these insurance shelters: the investor lets the interest—now about 7 per cent—accumulate tax-free until it's withdrawn at retirement, presumably at a lower tax bracket.

    An approach worth looking at: Suppose your home is mortgage-free, and you're ten years from retirement and in the 50 per cent bracket. Consider a new ten-year mortgage, say for $50,000. Payments at 9 per cent would total $76,000 over ten years, but $26,000 of that would be tax-deductible interest, so your interest cost would be only $13,000. If the $50,000 proceeds were invested in a deferred annuity at 7-1/4 per cent, you'd have $100,000 in your annuity and a paid-up mortgage at retirement.

3. *Series E.* Even U.S. Savings Bonds can shelter income. The trade-off for the safety of the government guarantee is a relatively low 6 per cent interest rate. Series E bonds mature in five years, but investors can continue earning tax-deferred interest rather than cashing them in. At retirement, bondholders can cash E bonds in each year to provide partly taxable income, or they can convert to H bonds, which pay semiannual taxable interest.

§7.07

HOW DO YOU SPELL SUCCESS?

Many ventures we have not discussed also provide excellent opportunities for generating large tax-sheltered sums. But all of them carry with them the potential for financial disaster. To avoid the avoidable pitfalls, a project obviously must make sense from both legal and accounting vantage points. In addition, it must be coordinated and directed by a knowledgeable and experienced promoter—a professional. The sound leadership and integrity offered by this professional will give you the extra edge you need to achieve tax-sheltered success.

CHAPTER 8

AVOIDING MALPRACTICE LITIGATION

§8.01

WHY NOW?

Malpractice brings thoughts of malevolent incompetence to the public's mind. As a professional, you should know better. Professional negligence is not the bane of the underskilled or incautious practitioner alone. In this age of consumerism, even the most knowledgeable and thorough health professionals are compelled to practice "defensively." They are performing additional tests and carrying out additional diagnostic procedures, just to be on the safe side of any eventual malpractice suit. Only fifteen years ago, a negligence claim against a health professional was a rarity. Today they're almost taken for granted. Why?

One answer looks away from the profession, and blames greedy patients and lawyers who stir up litigation. Regrettably, too much fact supports the thesis.

Another explanation cites the evolution of health care in the United States. The rise of specialization has left patients with an unfulfilled need for warm personal attention, and at the same time has heightened their expectations. If health care science is now so exact, nothing should ever go wrong, not in this Marcus Welby world of thirty-minute absolute solutions to medical problems. If something does go wrong, there may be less reluctance to take action against someone who isn't a family "friend" of long standing.

The use of powerful new drugs has also contributed to the dilemma. Health professionals don't universally acquaint their patients with all the risks of medication, and patients may remember words of warning selectively. Both can lead to dissatisfaction.

Finally, health care has now moved beyond the basics. A patient can elect cosmetic surgery, for instance, and get fighting mad about subjectively poor results.

§8.02

HELP IS ON THE WAY

Despite the large number of substantial settlements and awards that seem to have been made recently, it is not very likely that you will be sued. The odds are about one in a thousand that any doctor-patient encounter will end up in court. Most cases that do get that far see their doctor defendants vindicated. Much of the publicity results from the sad fact that those few who do lose, lose big, in money and in reputation.

If you are a specializing M.D., the odds that litigation will involve you are lower, and so are your chances at trial. It is no secret that these groups are the most likely to be sued:

1. Orthopedic surgeons
2. Anesthesiologists
3. General surgeons
4. Obstetricians and gynecologists
5. General practitioners and internists

Many doctors feel it is unfair that one mistake can end a career. They see a marked lack of restraint in an occasional medical blunder costing society at large hundreds of millions of dollars every year in increased health costs and insurance premiums.

Fortunately, the "malpractice crisis" is cooling down. Doctors are no longer running scared, and need not look on every patient as a potential legal adversary. There are some good reasons for this trend.

1. More and more, binding arbitration is working. At the start of their relationship, a patient and his doctor or hospital can sign an agreement to bring any future malpractice claim to an arbitration board and agree to accept its decision. Arbitration is an effective way to ease crowded court calendars, to cut the time between claim and settlement, and to assure the injured parties of a larger share of the monetary award than they'd otherwise keep. It's also an efficient way for doctors to prove their innocence, without years of agony and legal technicalities seeming to block every move.

2. Judges are creatively trying to replace huge, lump-sum awards with reason. One alternative is the "reversionary trust." In this situation, a responsible defendant would be called upon to fund a trust large enough to pay out sufficient interest to meet the financial needs of a wronged patient and his family. After the patient dies and his children grow up, the trust could be terminated, and the principal would revert to the defendant. Surely this is fairer than transforming the plaintiff's heirs into "instant millionaires," should he die soon after a $1 million verdict is returned.

3. Many doctors and hospitals are paying less for malpractice insurance than they did last year. Some have pooled their resources and formed their own "offshore captive" insurance companies in Bermuda or the Caribbean, where they escape state insurance regulations and where capitalization requirements are lower. Others are forming "domestic captives" or setting up private trust funds. Still others are buying legal defense coverage alone or "going bare" altogether. They're playing the odds, knowing that they'll probably never be sued and, if they are, that they'll probably win.

4. Legislation is starting to help, too. Many states have reduced the time limits within which malpractice suits must be brought. Insurance companies are being forced to substantiate their premium demands, and plaintiffs are being held statutorily liable for expenses and attorneys' fees when they initiate unfounded suits.

5. Groups are being formed to aid in fighting frivolous claims through countersuits, and they're rapidly gaining the support of those thousands of lawyers who acknowledge their responsibility to participate only in meritorious causes.

§8.03

WHAT IS MALPRACTICE?

Progress notwithstanding, doctors must protect themselves, and the best way to protect themselves is to protect their patients. The thought will hit home after we investigate the real meaning of malpractice, and where it is likely to come up in your practice.

Malpractice is simply negligence, no more and no less. Its proof (in theory, at least) is not very different from proving the facts of an auto accident, although there are peculiar subtleties and the stakes are a whole lot higher. These are the elements any plaintiff must prove in any garden-variety negligence case:

1. *The duty element.* The defendant owed a duty to the plaintiff.
2. *The breach element.* The defendant breached that duty.
3. *The contributory negligence element.* The plaintiff himself was not negligent.
4. *The causation element.* The defendant's breach of duty was the "direct and proximate" cause of a result.
5. *The damages element.* That result was a legally cognizable injury to the plaintiff.

So far, so good. That legalese could use some translating, however. Let's turn the theory into a few practical definitions:

1. *The duty element.* The basic idea is that you are held to a certain standard of conduct. You owe it to your patients to perform at the level they reasonably expect of a doctor. Society insists on that kind of performance. Let us break it down further:

§8.04

OBTAIN CONSENT

(a) *That you treat at all.* Before you treat, get your patients' *informed consent.* Tell them what you plan to do and why, what results you expect, what risks are present, what side effects are in the offing, all the alternatives—and get their O.K. Otherwise, you are assaulting your patients—and assault is relatively easy for them to prove!

§8.05

EMERGENCIES

The obvious exception is the *emergency* situation. If, for instance, during the course of an operation, a surgeon finds a serious and immediate danger to the patient's health but, as a practical matter, cannot gain consent, it is all right to go ahead and remedy the danger. We say that consent is *implied* by the circumstances.

§8.06

LIVING UP TO STANDARDS

(b) *How you treat.* The standards we're talking about here are professional standards and community standards. When do you call in a specialist? What diagnostic aids do you use? When do you release a patient? These kinds of issues are not decided in a vacuum. Compare your practice with those of others in your locality, for that is how a court goes about defining your duty to your patients.

§8.07

BEING CAREFUL

(c) *How well you treat.* Direct misconduct is always a breach of duty, so you are always obligated to exercise common sense. It's a surgeon's duty not to leave a scalpel in the operative field, and not to operate on the wrong patient or the wrong organ. It is any doctor's duty to follow a drug manufacturer's standard, rather than overdosing a patient. In short, it is your duty to be *careful*, and no patient consents to carelessness.

2. *The breach element.* There are sins of omission and sins of commission. Once a court has defined your duty, you are held to it. Not only must you perform, if that is your mandate, but also you must perform well. Otherwise, you have not met your legal obligation to your patient, and a court will usually decide that way even if the patient has signed an *exculpatory agreement*, a prior release of any negligence.

§8.08

YOUR PATIENT'S OBLIGATION

3. *The contributory negligence element.* Suppose your patient charges you with recklessly administering 25 mg of a drug the manufacturer has clearly labeled "SUGGESTED DOSAGE: 10 mg." It looks like you are on the hook. On the other hand, what if the patient took another 10 mg on his own, without your approval? He negligently contributed to whatever ill effect resulted, and his case probably ought to be thrown out of court.

In some states, the plaintiff must demonstrate he was not negligent. In others, the defendant must demonstrate he was. (Courts in "comparative negligence" states take a different tack: if both the plaintiff and defendant were negligent, the person *more* at fault must be held accountable.) Who has the *burden of proof* makes an important difference. The more your adversary must prove, the less you must prove and the easier time you will have.

§8.09

DISCOVERY

4. *The causation element.* Malpractice trials are based on events that precede them by years. It is difficult to imagine how a plaintiff's lawyer, never in the operating room or at the treatment site, can reconstruct what happened for the jury's benefit and prove that a specific injury was caused just as alleged. Yet it can be done.

Years earlier he will have intensively *discovered* the case—learned everything there was to learn through written *interrogatories* and oral *depositions.* Even the defendant's own pretrial statement is taken with a view toward using it against him or her. Ultimately, in court, causation is proved. Here's how:

§8.10

BRING IN THE EXPERTS

(a) *Expert testimony.* The opinion of a medical witness can carry a good deal of weight in showing exactly how an injury occurred. Rules of evidence demand that the testimony of any experts be founded in what they themselves know. They can state facts, but not guesses or legal opinions. If a plaintiff's witness examined the plaintiff at the time of the defendant's supposed malpractice, evidentiary requirements are easily satisfied. The witness can surely testify about something he or she knows firsthand.

But suppose the witness is brought in after the fact. Is his or her testimony admissable? It can be. That's where the so-called "hypothetical" question is powerfully employed against doctor-defendants. Plaintiff's counsel takes *all* the relevant evidence and builds it into a long "hypothetical" question, calculated to prove causation:

Counsel: "If the plaintiff suffered symptoms x, y, and z, and if tests A, B, and C showed results K and L, and if then the defendant failed to perform procedure P, based on a reasonable degree of scientific certainty, do you have an opinion as to whether condition Q would have thereby resulted?"
Witness: "Yes, I do."
Counsel: "And what is that opinion?"
Witness: "Condition Q would have resulted."

Consider the tactical advantage: the plaintiff has summed up all the facts he thinks he proved, and liability becomes an obvious conclusion. It is true that an expert's testimony as to possibilities cannot carry the day; however, when that testimony is corroborated by a barrage of other evidence, the inference inescapably arises that your breach of duty was causally linked to your patient's complained injury.

Your lawyer will challenge the relevance of the hypothetical question. It must contain only the facts that have been established and all of them. If it does not, your lawyer can add to it or delete from it, and try to sway the witness to your side.

§8.11

WHERE NEGLIGENCE IS OBVIOUS

(b) *Res ipsa loquitur.* Sometimes the plaintiff does not even need an expert witness, because any layman knows that certain results can *only* occur through negligence. Res ipsa loquitur means "the thing speaks for itself." It's a doctrine that makes short work of the causation proof.

Take the patient who leaves the operating room, a sponge sutured within, and then sues everyone who had any connection with the surgery:

(i) The accident is not the kind that normally occurs in the absence of negligence.

(ii) The accident was caused by an instrumentality exclusively within the defendants' control.

(iii) The accident was not the fault of the patient.

In short, *res ispa loquitur*; by the few facts we know, the plaintiff has met the burden of proving causation. Now it's up to each defendant to argue where the flaw lies.

§8.12

"YES, I WAS NEGLIGENT — BUT SO WHAT?"

5. *The damages element.* If you were negligent, how much injury, in dollars, did your negligence cause? The sympathy factor is commonly a significant one, but a *technical battery,* for example, one in which the plaintiff is not provably injured, just isn't compensable.

§8.13

WHEN YOU HAVE NO DEFENSE

Too often, tragically, all the elements appear to be present—a duty, its breach, and the direct and exclusive causation of a patient's injury. A person who devotes his life to healing and soothing, ironically, has caused pain and suffering. Groping for forgiveness, he may offer testimony. Should you ever enter that personal hell of a malpractice suit, know that cries for compassion are *not defenses* and know why.

- *You meant well.* You did not follow a recognized technique, or you departed from what is thought to be "proper" practice. That is what counts. If your intentions were the highest and your reputation is otherwise stellar, the fact nonetheless remains. You are guilty of malpractice.
- *Even if you had employed a recognized technique, the patient would have died—or lost his leg—or gone blind—or [fill in the blank].* You did not, however, and your conjecture about what might have been will not help now.
- *The patient was so sick!* The treatment of the ill is a responsibility you willingly undertook, not a risk that was foisted upon you. Your patient's condition called for reasonable care; you are simply liable for any failure to give it.

§8.14

DEFENSES THAT WORK

Let's not be unduly hard on you, the doctor. You honorably devote your time to the care of the sick and practice your profession as well as you can. However, you are only human, and, almost inevitably, you will make a mistake—one that causes a patient to suffer. Your reputation can be devastated, your personal wealth appropriated. For future reference, note these defenses. They have saved more than one illustrious career:

- *The statute of limitations.* Usually, the plaintiff's case must be filed within two years after the negligence occurred, or the plaintiff is forever barred from suing. Many statutes have been liberalized to permit plaintiffs to sue later, if they could not reasonably have known about the negligence within two years.
- *A defective complaint.* If the plaintiff is claiming your treatment led to a bad result, that is not negligence. You are not an insurer of absolute success.
- *The wrong defendant.* If you were the anesthesiologist in the operating room when the general surgeon neglected to remove the sponge from his patient, any suit against you should not hold up.
- *Assumed risk.* Sure, you tried an unorthodox procedure, and yes, it failed. Your patient suffered irreparable harm. You told him that was a danger, however, and he said, "Give it a try." He bore the risk, not you.

- *Contributory negligence.* As an optometrist you recognized the signs of glaucoma and strongly advised your patient to visit an ophthalmologist without delay. He said he would make an appointment, but never did—until he started losing his sight. He cannot blame you now for failing to follow through on that visit to an M.D. Your patient took the matter out of your hands, and only he can be blamed for his plight.
- *Active negligence versus passive negligence.* As a primary physician, perhaps you should have looked more closely at the findings of a consultant. You did not, however, and the consultant was wrong. Your patient suffered injury from that error and sues you. In some states, your defense can be, "I was negligent, but only passively. Charges should be brought against the one who really committed the error, the consultant."

§8.15

HOW ANOTHER'S NEGLIGENCE BECOMES YOURS

The matter of defense is all the more complicated when you are alleged to be liable for the negligence of other professionals. Usually, you are not responsible for the acts of other doctors, but these exceptions are clear:

1. As a generalist, you are liable for the negligence of a "specialist" if you didn't exercise care in selecting him or her.
2. You are liable for the negligence of your partner.
3. You are liable for the negligence of your agent. If you do not have time to perform the surgery and send Dr. Phillips instead, Dr. Phillips' negligence is yours.
4. By the "Captain of the Ship" principle, in a few states you may be liable for the negligence of any doctor working under you. Thus, the anesthesiologist's negligence is imputed to the surgeon in charge.

With an almost infinite variety of potential liability patterns, and with the undeserved popularity of the "spectrum" suit (naming as a defendant everybody in sight), one may well feel helpless. How can you protect yourself?

§8.16

WHERE THE MALPRACTICE BUG THRIVES

First, find your Achilles' heel. Most malpractice actions focus on one of the few areas in which doctors are most vulnerable. Make sure you are not open to a lawsuit based on one of these potent theories:

- *Unnecessary surgery.* Document the reason that surgery is required, and invite your patient to seek corroboration of your opinion. The same goes for therapy of any kind.
- *No informed consent.* Tell your patient about all the risks any proposed treatment or surgery poses. Get your patient's signature (or his guardian's, if he's a minor) on a consent form, or have a witness present when you get the go-ahead. Better still, do both.
- *Assault.* When you gain your patient's authorization to perform surgery, obtain consent for any related procedure you might find necessary.
- *Abandonment.* Do not go on that extended vacation after you leave the operating room unless you are adequately covered by another competent doctor, one you have told your patient about. Document any premature termination of your doctor-patient relationship. The American Medical Association suggests that form letters like the following be executed, with copies retained indefinitely with the patient's records.

LETTER OF WITHDRAWAL FROM CASE

Dear Mr._____:

I find it necessary to inform you I am withdrawing from further professional attendance upon you for the reason that you have persisted in refusing to follow my medical advice and treatment. Since your condition requires medical attention, I suggest that you place yourself under the care of another physician without delay. If you so desire, I shall be available to attend you for a reasonable time after you have received this letter, but in no event for more than five days.

This should give you ample time to select a physician of your choice from the many competent practitioners in this city. With your approval, I will make available to this physician your case history and information regarding the diagnosis and treatment which you have received from me.

Very truly yours,

_____

Adapted from Medicolegal Forms with Legal Analysis, 3rd ed. Office of the General Counsel, American Medical Association, 1973.

LETTER TO CONFIRM DISCHARGE BY PATIENT

Dear Mr. _____ :

This will confirm our telephone conversation of today in which you discharged me from attending you as your physician in your present illness. In my opinion your condition requires continued medical treatment by a physician. If you have not already done so, I suggest that you employ another physician without delay. You may be assured that, at your request, I will furnish him with information regarding the diagnosis and treatment which you have received from me.

Very truly yours,

_____

Adapted from Medicolegal Forms with Legal Analysis, 3rd ed. Office of the General Counsel, American Medical Association, 1973.

STATEMENT OF PATIENT LEAVING
HOSPITAL AGAINST ADVICE

This is to certify that I am leaving _____
Hospital at my own insistence and against the advice of
the hospital authorities and my attending physician. I
have been informed by them of the dangers of my
leaving the hospital at this time. I release the hospital, its
employees and officers, and my attending physician from
all liability for any adverse results caused by my leaving
the hospital prematurely.

Signed _____

I agree to hold harmless the _____
Hospital, its employees and officers, and the attending
physician from all liability, with reference to the
discharge of the patient named above.

_____
(Husband, wife, parent, etc.)

Date _____

Witness _____

Adapted from Medicolegal Forms with Legal Analysis, 3rd ed. Office
of the General Counsel, American Medical Association, 1973.

LETTER TO PATIENT WHO FAILS TO KEEP APPOINTMENT

Dear Mr. _____ :

On _____ , 19_____ , you failed to keep
your appointment at my office. In my opinion your
condition requires continued medical treatment. If you so
desire, you may telephone me for another appointment,
but if you prefer to have another physician attend you, I
suggest that you arrange to do so without delay. You
may be assured that, at your request, I am entirely
willing to make available my knowledge of your case to
the physician of your choice.

I trust that you will understand that my purpose in
writing this letter is out of concern for your health and
well-being.

Very truly yours,

_____

Adapted from Medicolegal Forms with Legal Analysis, 3rd ed.
Office of the General Counsel, American Medical Association, 1973.

LETTER TO PATIENT WHO FAILS TO FOLLOW ADVICE

Dear Mr._____ :

At the time that you brought you son, William, to me for examination this afternoon, I informed you that I was unable to determine without X-ray pictures whether a fracture existed in his injured right arm. I strongly urge you to permit me or some other physician of your choice to make this X-ray examination without further delay.

Your neglect in not permitting a proper X-ray examination to be made of William's right arm may result in serious consequences if in fact a fracture does exist.

Very truly yours,

_____

Adapted from Medicolegal Forms with Legal Analysis, 3rd ed. Office of the General Counsel, American Medical Association, 1973.

§8.17

PROTECTING YOURSELF

Heed these few final hints, and you will sleep better tonight:

[See Chapter 9]
[See §12.09]

- Clinicians must keep good records, both at the hospital and at the office. Detailed notes, verified by an aide, become invaluable defense evidence at trial.
- Keep your equipment current and well-maintained. Its error is yours.
- Insure yourself. A $1,000,000 malpractice policy, in addition to an umbrella policy for professional and personal liability, is not unrealistic.
- Make sure any hospital at which you work properly checks credentials. Associating yourself with an unqualified practitioner invites trouble.
- Do not be an innovator unless you are a researcher by profession. Before trying a new procedure, be certain it is supported by literature in your field and acknowledged by your colleagues.
- Be part of a team when you can. Consult with experts in a coordinated way, and you will enjoy the combined brainpower of the group. You will also have developed backup support for your conclusions.
- Use all the data you can gather. If you are a radiologist, for instance, and administrative policy permits, do not read X-rays without seeing a history or reviewing a chart. There's no wisdom in knowingly bypassing an existing source of information.
- When something inadvertently goes wrong, tell your patient or his family fast and frankly. Candor can sometimes nip litigation in the bud.

§8.18

WHAT TO DO IF YOU ARE SUED

Practice defensively, and keep your standards as high as possible. Should you be sued, you will have reason to stay cool. Let this be your strategy:

[See §12.09]

1. Notify your insurance company as soon as you think you might be sued.
2. Do not think your insurer will totally protect your interest; beyond the limits of your policy, you are on your own. So notify your lawyer at once, too, and be patient. The lawyer will need time to prepare a credible defense.
3. Do not discuss your case with anyone else, except at a deposition when your lawyer will be present. Sometimes, a statement made to the lawyer for a codefendant hospital, for example, is held against a doctor once he or she is in court.
4. Let your local professional society in on your problem. It is a good source for expert witnesses to testify on your behalf, as well as for moral support.
5. If you are at fault, settle quickly, before the plaintiff's lawyer has put in too many hours and cannot justify a low settlement. You will avoid a pretrial examination, which is bound to be a burden to you and your staff, not to mention the loss in time and fees.
6. If all else fails, sit back and let your lawyer go to work. Seek solace in the fact that any doctor can become involved in a malpractice battle, and you did all in your power to minimize the consequences.

§8.19

LEARN A LESSON

Remember, even a verdict in your favor does not make a malpractice defendant a winner. Any litigation, even if it is baseless, can be a shattering blow to your reputation. Treat your practice like a tightly run business, and you are more than likely to avoid a terrifying and scarring experience.

CHAPTER 9

TO BUY OR TO LEASE?

§9.01

THE DILEMMA IN BRIEF

The average health professional spends a hefty portion of total income on professional equipment. Generally, one may choose to buy or to lease. Some contend that it is really no choice at all. Why tie up productive capital in a piece of machinery when you can lease instead and deduct your entire rental costs? Since money is continually losing its value, the anti-inflationary character of fixed payments sounds tremendously appealing, too. Add a few tax pluses and the beauty of avoiding an ownership right in unwanted, obsolescent equipment years from now, and leasing seems ideal.

Just when you have made up your mind that leasing must be the answer, some happy purchaser is bound to remind you that depreciation and interest are tax-deductible. When you *buy* your equipment, you are sure to make out better on your federal income tax return. Besides, do you really think you would want to trade in that shiny, ultramodern machinery in less than six or eight years?

§9.02

LEASE VERSUS PURCHASE

Now you are more puzzled than ever, so let us take first things first. The odds are your decision will be based partly on the tax planning considerations we will explore. Whatever you decide, you will be sorely disappointed if your "lease " turns out to be a purchase, or your "purchase" a lease. Learn how to tell a sales contract from a lease agreement, and bear in mind that what the vendor has labeled the document you sign will not be dispositive when the IRS takes a look at it.

Problems occur most often when health professionals seek the middle road in a lease with a purchase option. The theory is unbeatable: keep your equipment current forever, write off your contract payments as soon as you make them, and free your capital for other uses. Make sure you know what you are doing, however. Scrutinize that "lease"; too many of these telltale clues mean you have a full-fledged sales contract on your desk:

- The contract talks about the tax advantages you will enjoy.
- Title to the equipment is to go into escrow.
- You will own the equipment as soon as the lease term is over.
- You are going to be held responsible for maintenance and repairs from Day One.
- The equipment is expected to be useful far beyond the term of the lease.

- The option price is surprisingly small, given the equipment's value.
- The monthly contract payments plus the option price just happen to equal the equipment's purchase price and some reasonable rate of interest.

§9.03

THE ADVANTAGES OF LEASING

We have said that the IRS might take your "lease" and call it a "purchase," if it looks like one, and we have implied that somehow a purchase is bad. Well, maybe. At least for some health professionals, a lease offers opportunities a purchase simply cannot:

- For one thing, you have saved that big capital outlay.
- You are buying the use of whatever new equipment you want with tax-deductible dollars.
- Your investment will not decline in value. When it does not serve your purpose anymore, call the leasing company and have the equipment taken away. Finding a buyer becomes someone else's problem.
- All the while, your credit lines stay open and available for other investments.

§9.04

THE PURCHASE LEASE-BACK

Sometimes leasing is so irresistible that many health professionals will sell equipment they have already bought just to lease it back. A "purchase lease-back" is a beautiful tax-shelter; buy an X-ray machine outright, for instance. You will deduct first-year depreciation, which might represent a major part of the purchase price, you will recall. Deduct another 20 per cent of so-called "bonus" depreciation if the asset you are buying has a useful life of six years or more. If you are borrowing the purchase money, also deduct your interest expense. A year later, have your X-ray unit appraised and sell it—at its fair market value—to a leasing company. You will get back the lion's share of the price you paid, and you will enter into a lease allowing you to continue using your equpment. Reinvest the capital that has been returned to you, and deduct all your lease payments as they are made. This looks like the best of all possible worlds.

§9.05

THE AUTO LEASE

Without question, the most popular equipment lease around is the auto lease. There are three kinds, and one of them might make sense for you:

1. *The finance lease.* Pay a really low monthly charge, but be responsible if your car is not in first-rate condition at the end of the two-year lease term.
2. *The net lease.* Pay a little more each month, and avoid the possibility of a big cash outlay for normal wear and tear.
3. *The maintenance lease.* Pay still more and you will even have servicing costs included in your monthly payments.

You may want to jettison the old notion that building up "equity" is a worthwhile goal. Lease your car, and here's how you will gain:

- First, dispense with the frustration of shopping and haggling. Unless you are really a combination auto buff and negotiator of the first order, that's good news.
- The big expense that is spelled C-A-R is easier to take in little doses. No longer need you write a check for $6,000 or $8,000 every couple of years.
- "Trading in" becomes easy. You'll get your old car's Red Book value (minus the cost of necessary repairs), and you will get it in cash and in front.
- Auto insurance may be cheaper. You can probably participate in a group plan.
- You will keep the IRS happy. The cost of operating your car can be easily computed and substantiated. After all, your lease payments are fixed.
- For the same reason, you will easily budget your transportation costs, especially important if you have incorporated.
- A happy ending: at the lease's conclusion, you might be able to buy your car for $50 or $100 off wholesale.

§9.06

PURCHASING HAS SOME POINTS

On balance, leasing—a car or anything else, for that matter—is not always better than purchasing. Make your decision the same way you make any other investment decision, and remember the pro's of purchasing:

- When you buy equipment, the equipment is all you need to pay for. Contrast that with a lease, inevitably laden with finance charges. You know you can borrow money cheaper from your bank than you can from your lessor.
- Interest is fully tax-deductible.
- When you buy, you're getting what you bargained for—the equipment. When you lease, you might also be assuming some hidden risks. A purchase lease-back arrangement, for instance, carries with it a tax-shelter, and tax-shelters are not always profitable. Even if yours is, watch out for *recaptured depreciation*. Any gain you realize on the sale of certain depreciable property is taxed as ordinary income to the extent of the depreciation you deducted. Consequently, your lease falls short of sheltered perfection. The fast write-off you dreamed about is brought right back into your income and taxed all the way up to the 70 per cent bracket.
- When you buy, you can deduct depreciation. In fact, depreciation can be just as tax-reducing as lease payments—more so, sometimes, because depreciation deductions can be taken more or less as you need them. In addition, do not forget that 20 per cent first-year "bonus" depreciation.

§9.07

THE INVESTMENT TAX CREDIT

Whether you buy or purchase, take advantage of the 10 per cent investment credit, if you can. Briefly, here's how this incentive for modernization in your practice works:

1. For the credit to apply at all, you must be investing in *qualified property*. That means new property or used property—but at most, $100,000 of the cost of used property is eligible. Property with a useful life of less than three years does not qualify, and neither does "sale and lease-back" property. Otherwise, just about any other kind of depreciable, tangible personal property—but not most buildings—qualifies.

2. How much credit is yours depends on the property's *useful life*—the same life that applies to your depreciation. If the property has a useful life of three or four years, 1/3 of your investment is taken to compute your tax credit. If the property has a useful life of five or six years, 2/3 is taken. If the property's useful life is at least seven years, the entire cost is taken.

3. Just multiply the applicable factor by 10 per cent, and that is your credit.

4. Claim the credit the year your property is placed in service. If you are purchasing, that is the year your equipment is ready for use or the first year you can take depreciation—whichever is earlier. If you are leasing, claim your credit the year you have assumed possession of the property or the first year it can be depreciated—again, whichever is earlier. Note, however, that you may only claim the credit if the lessor has waived it; refer to your lease on this point.

5. What if you sell your property before its useful life is over, or what if it loses its qualification? *Recapture* happens. The difference between the credit you've claimed and the credit that is justly yours is taxed to you. That is shown on Form 3468.

The investment credit is not a deduction; it is a direct credit against your tax liability, and one more potentially volatile factor you ought to consider when you elect to purchase or to lease. The inquiry is always a complex one. Grant it the deliberation it obviously deserves.

Form **3468**
Department of the Treasury
Internal Revenue Service

Computation of Investment Credit

▶ Attach to your tax return.

19--

Name

Diligent Doctor

Identifying number as shown on page 1 of your tax return

123 - 45 - 6789

1 Use schedule below to list qualified investment in new and used property acquired or constructed and placed in service during the taxable year; and also list qualified progress expenditures made during the 19-- taxable year and qualified progress expenditures made in 19--, 19--, and 19-- taxable years providing a proper election as prescribed in section 46(d)(6) was made for such prior years. If progress expenditure property is placed in service during the taxable year, do not list qualified progress expenditures for this property. See instruction for line 1.

If 100% investment credit is being claimed on certain ships, check this block. ▶ ☐ See Instruction K for details.

Note: *Include your share of investment in property made by a partnership, estate, trust, small business corporation, or lessor.*

Type of property		Line	(1) Life years	(2) Cost or basis (See instruction G)	(3) Applicable percentage	(4) Qualified investment (Column 2 x column 3)
New property		(a)	3 or more but less than 5	3,224	33⅓	1,075
		(b)	5 or more but less than 7		66⅔	
		(c)	7 or more	1,500	100	1,500
Qualified progress expenditures	three prior years	(d)	7 or more		20	
	this year	(e)	7 or more		60	
Used property (See instructions for dollar limitation)		(f)	3 or more but less than 5		33⅓	
		(g)	5 or more but less than 7		66⅔	
		(h)	7 or more		100	

2 Qualified investment—add lines 1(a) through (h) . . . . | 2,575

3 10% of line 2 . . . . | 258

4 7% (4% for public utility property) of certain property (see instruction for line 1) . . . . |

5 Corporations electing the additional investment credit for contributions to Employee Stock Ownership Plans—Attach election statement. (See Instruction I and instruction for line 5.)
  (a) Additional 1% credit—Enter 1% of line 2 . . . . |

  (b) Additional credit not to exceed .5%—Enter allowable percentage times adjusted line 2 (attach schedule) . . . . |

6 Carryback and carryover of unused credit(s). See Instruction F—attach computation . . . . |

7 Tentative investment credit—Add lines 3 through 6 . . . . | 258

Limitation

8 (a) Individuals—Enter amount from line 37, page 2, Form 1040 . . . . . . ⎫
  (b) Estates and trusts—Enter amount from line 26 or 27, page 1, Form 1041 . . . ⎬ . . . | 5,831
  (c) Corporations—Enter amount from line 9, Schedule J, page 3, Form 1120 . . . . ⎭

9 (a) Credit for the elderly (individuals only) . . . . |

  (b) Foreign tax credit . . . . |

  (c) Tax on lump-sum distributions (see instruction for line 9(c)) . . . . |

  (d) Possession Tax Credit (corporations only) . . . . |

  (e) Section 72(m)(5) penalty tax . . . . |

10 Total—Add lines 9(a) through (e) . . . . |

11 Line 8 less line 10 . . . . | 5,831

12 (a) Enter amount on line 11 or $25,000, whichever is lesser. (Married persons filing separately, controlled corporate groups, estates, and trusts, see instruction for line 12.) . . . . | 5,831

  (b) If line 11 exceeds line 12(a), enter 50% of the excess. (Public utilities, railroads, and airlines, see Instruction J.) . . . . |

13 Total—Add lines 12(a) and (b) . . . . | 5,831

14 Investment credit—Amount from line 7 or line 13, whichever is lesser. Enter here and on line 41, Form 1040; line 10(b), Schedule J, page 3, Form 1120; or the appropriate line on other returns . . . . . | 258

Schedule A If any part of your investment in line 1 or 4 above was made by a partnership, estate, trust, small business corporation, or lessor, complete the following statement and identify property qualifying for the 7% or 10% investment credit.

Name (Partnership, estate, trust, etc.)	Address	Property			
		Progress expenditures	New	Used	Life years
		$	$	$	

If property is disposed of prior to the life years used in computing the investment credit, see Instruction E.

Form **3468** (19--)

CHAPTER **10**

YOUR ROLE AS A CREDITOR

§10.01

THE ECONOMIC REALITY

It may be an unalterable fact of your business life that your professional relationship with your patients and the creditor-debtor relationship must coexist. Your charge system, your billing and collection procedure, and your insurance processing method must assure the continuing financial stability of your practice. At the same time, they must sensitively respond to your patients' needs and expectations.

The determination of fees has never been an easy matter. While a humanitarian preoccupation with a patient's ability to pay has historically complicated professional decision-making, the trend today is toward competitive scheduled fees. Blue Cross and Blue Shield and union welfare plans publish schedules, keeping the public knowledgeable about "average" fees nationwide. Large group practices tend to serve specific socio-economic groups, in which the ability to pay isn't much of a variable; and more insurance plans than ever before—Medicare, Medicaid, and the Maternal and Child Health Programs among them—are increasing patients' medical buying power while promulgating standard benefit schedules.

The frequent result is reliance on relative value studies in the establishment of reasonable fee charges. Consider developing a standard fee schedule by applying cost-based monetary values to a recent relative value survey, adjusted for profit and a reserve for future practice growth.

§10.02

A CREDIT POLICY

However your charges are established, do all you can to bill and collect all that is rightfully yours. To that end, this policy is worth adopting:

- Extend enough credit so that your insurance- and savings-poor patients can get the treatment they need when they need it.
- Be specific with your patients. Make sure they understand what they're supposed to pay and when.
- Categorize your patients so your staff can effectively administer the collection effort. There is a difference between the patient who simply can't pay and the patient who can but won't.

- Develop a firm attitude about collections that will translate into the profits you need to stay safely afloat, but that won't turn satisfied patients away needlessly.

Many offices are now committing their credit policies to writing. Misunderstandings can thus be avoided, and defaults can more easily be remedied. What's more, the federal Truth in Lending Act now requires that you disclose any finance charge, in both dollars and annual percentage rate. Even when no interest is charged, a patient who agrees to pay the bill in four or more installments brings you within the Act's scope.

It's a good idea to post your credit policy in your business office, to distribute informational brochures when patients check in, and to restate your financial policy on billing statements. It's also good Truth in Lending compliance.

FINANCIAL INFORMATION

Estimate of charges:

New patients are invited to request estimates of charges prior to laboratory and X-ray work. This will give you an opportunity to see what tests are scheduled and their estimated cost. You may request an estimate of charges at any time—now or on future visits.

Insurance:

If you have insurance information to submit, our receptionist will assist you. We ask that you pay us directly and allow your insurance company to reimburse you.

Payment:

We ask new patients to understand our payment policy. If you are not in a position to pay our charges at the time our services are performed, the balance will be payable within ten days of receipt of your first statement. Should you wish to discuss finances, please let our receptionist know.

In nonemergency situations, information should flow both ways, especially if charges are based on your patients' ability to pay them. Before services are rendered, you may want to order an investigation and see that a confidential interview is conducted in your office. You'll learn:

1. The patient's full name.
2. The patient's current and immediate past home address, and whether the property is owned or rented.
3. The patient's (and spouse's) occupation and employer.
4. The patient's insurance carrier and policy number.
5. The name and addresses of personal and credit references.

Financially troubled patients can be identified and asked to pay as services are rendered or on target progress-payment dates. You may require a third-party guarantor, or even refuse to undertake a nonemergency procedure. If it comes to a confrontation, the data your interview assembles will prove invaluable in the enforcement of your rights.

§10.03

SEEKING OUTSIDE HELP

Those patients who enjoy the privilege of credit deserve prompt, fair, and accurately itemized statements. Systematic thoroughness clearly enhances collection success. Only after a series of unheeded reminders should you consider further action, including referral to a collection agency.

Before a collection agency is retained, investigate it carefully:

- Any collection agency you hire must be licensed and bonded.
- It should be scrupulously ethical, shunning harsh and abusive tactics and declining to share confidential information with retail creditors.
- The agency should be pleased to furnish references from your colleagues.
- It should be near you geographically, and ready and able to confer with you and your staff.
- Finally, a professional agency probably should be able to collect 30 to 60 per cent of the accounts you assign it, and should charge you no more than half of what it collects. Demand results.

§10.04

MEDICARE, MEDICAID, AND MORE

Fortunately, the timely collection of fees isn't the problem it once was. More patients than ever are insured against medical expenses. Government insurance programs alone pay nearly half of our nation's health bill, so make it your business to understand Medicare hospital insurance—Part A, Medicare medical insurance—Part B, and Medicaid, the supplemental program using federal and local tax revenues to pay the medical expenses of low-income persons.

The Department of Health, Education and Welfare, Social Security Administration, Baltimore, Maryland 21235 periodically publishes *Your Medical Handbook*; it's yours for the asking, and it's a must for every health care provider's office. As more technical Medicare questions arise, consult your Medicare carrier.

The following state by state listing tells you which agencies handle Medicare claims.

WHO HANDLES YOUR PATIENT'S MEDICARE CLAIMS?

Alabama
Medicare
Blue Cross-Blue Shield of Alabama
930 South 20th Street
Birmingham, Alabama 35205

Alaska
Medicare
Aetna Life & Casualty
Crown Plaza
1500 S.W. First Avenue
Portland, Oregon 97201

Arizona
Medicare
Aetna Life & Casualty
Medicare Claim Administration
3010 West Fairmount Avenue
Phoenix, Arizona 85017

Arkansas
Medicare
Arkansas Blue Cross and Blue Shield
P.O. Box 1418
Little Rock, Arkansas 72203

California
Counties of Los Angeles, Orange, San Diego,
Ventura, San Bernadino, Imperial,
San Luis Obispo, Riverside, Santa Barbara:
Medicare
Occidental Life Insurance Company of
   California
Box 54905
Terminal Annex
Los Angeles, California 90051

Rest of state:
Medicare
Blue Shield of California
P.O. Box 7968, Rincon Annex
San Francisco, California 94120

Colorado
Medicare
Colorado Medical Service, Inc.
700 Broadway
Denver, Colorado 80203

Connecticut
Medicare
Connecticut General Life Insurance Co.
200 Pratt Street
Meriden, Connecticut 06450

Delaware
Medicare
Blue Cross and Blue Shield of Delaware
201 West 14th Street
Wilmington, Delaware 19899

District of Columbia
Medicare
Medical Service of D.C.
550-12th Street., S.W.
Washington, D.C. 20024

Florida
Counties of Dade, Monroe:
Medicare
Group Health, Inc.
P.O. Box 341370
Miami, Florida 33134

Rest of state:
Medicare
Blue Shield of Florida, Inc.
P.O. Box 2525
Jacksonville, Florida 32203

Georgia
The Prudential Insurance Co. of America
Medicare Part B
P.O. Box 95466
Executive Park Station
Atlanta, Georgia 30347

Hawaii
Medicare
Aetna Life & Casualty
P.O. Box 3947
Honolulu, Hawaii 96812

Idaho
Medicare
The Equitable Life Assurance Society
P.O. Box 8048
Boise, Idaho 83707

Illinois
Cook County:
Medicare Part B
Illinois Medical Service
P.O. Box 210
Chicago, Illinois 60690

Rest of state:
Medicare
CNA Insurance
Medicare Benefits Division
P.O. Box 910
Chicago, Illinois 60690

Indiana
Medicare Part B
120 West Market Street
Indianapolis, Indiana 46204

Iowa
Medicare
Iowa Medical Service
636 Grand
Des Moines, Iowa 50307

Kansas
Counties of Johnson, Wyandotte:
Medicare
Blue Shield of Kansas City
P.O. Box 169
Kansas City, Missouri 64141

Rest of state:
Medicare
Kansas Blue Shield
P.O. Box 239
Topeka, Kansas 66601

Kentucky
Medicare
Metropolitan Life Insurance Co.
1218 Harrodsburg Road
Lexington, Kentucky 40504

Louisiana
Medicare
Pan-American Life Insurance Co.
P.O. Box 60450
New Orleans, Louisiana 70160

Maine
Medicare
Union Mutual Life Insurance Co.
Box 4629
Portland, Maine 04112

Maryland
Counties of Montgomery, Prince Georges:
Medicare
Medical Service of D.C.
550-12th St., S.W.
Washington, D.C. 20024

Rest of state:
Maryland Blue Shield, Inc.
700 East Joppa Road
Towson, Maryland 21204

Massachusetts
Medicare
Blue Shield of Massachusetts, Inc.
P.O. Box 2194
Boston, Massachusetts 02106

Michigan
Medicare
Blue Shield of Michigan
P.O. Box 2201
Detroit, Michigan 48231

Minnesota
Counties of Anoka, Dakota, Filmore,
Goodhue, Hennepin, Houston, Olmstead,
Ramsey, Wabasha, Washington, Winona:
Medicare
The Travelers Insurance Co.
8120 Penn Avenue, South
Bloomington, Minnesota 55431

Rest of state:
Medicare
Blue Shield of Minnesota
P.O. Box 8899
Minneapolis, Minnesota 55404

Mississippi
Medicare
The Travelers Insurance Co.
P.O. Box 22545
Jackson, Mississippi 39205

Missouri
Counties of Andrew, Atchison, Bates,
Benton, Buchanan, Caldwell, Carroll,
Cass, Clay, Clinton, Daviess, DeKalb,
Gentry, Grundy, Harrison, Henry, Holt,
Jackson, Johnson, Lafayette, Livingston,
Mercer, Nodaway, Pettis, Platte, Ray,
St. Clair, Saline, Vernon, Worth:
Medicare
Blue Shield of Kansas City
P.O. Box 169
Kansas City, Missouri 64141

Rest of state:
Medicare
General American Life Insurance Co.
P.O. Box 505
St. Louis, Missouri 63166

Montana
Medicare
Montana Physicians' Service
P.O. Box 2510
Helena, Montana 59601

Nebraska
Medicare
Mutual of Omaha Insurance Co.
P.O. Box 456, Downtown Station
Omaha, Nebraska 68101

Nevada
Medicare
Aetna Life & Casualty
4600 Kietzke Lane
P.O. Box 7290
Reno, Nevada 89510

New Hampshire
Medicare
New Hampshire-Vermont
   Physician Service
Two Pillsbury Street
Concord, New Hampshire 03301

New Jersey
The Prudential Insurance Co. of America
P.O. Box 3000
Linwood, New Jersey 08221

New Mexico
Medicare
The Equitable Life Assurance Society
P.O. Box 3070, Station D
Albuquerque, New Mexico 87110

New York
Counties of Bronx, Columbia, Delaware,
Dutchess, Greene, Kings, Nassau,
New York, Orange, Putnam, Richmond,
Rockland, Suffolk, Sullivan, Ulster,
Westchester:
Medicare
Blue Cross-Blue Shield of Greater
   New York
P.O. Box 458
Murray Hill Station
New York, New York 10016

County of Queens:
Medicare
Group Health, Inc.
P.O. Box 233-Midtown Station
New York, New York 10018

Counties of Livingston, Monroe, Ontario,
Seneca, Wayne, Yates:
Medicare
Genesee Valley Medical Care, Inc.
41 Chestnut Street
Rochester, New York 14647

Counties of Allegany, Cattaraugus, Erie,
Genesee, Niagara, Orleans, Wyoming:
Medicare
Blue Shield of Western New York, Inc.
298 Main Street
Buffalo, New York 14202

Counties of Albany, Broome, Cayuga,
Chautauqua, Chemung, Chenango,
Clinton, Cortland, Essex, Franklin,
Fulton, Hamilton, Herkimer, Jefferson,
Lewis, Madison, Montgomery, Oneida,
Onondaga, Oswego, Otsego, Rensselaer,
Saratoga, Schenectady, Schoharie,
Schuyler, Steuben, St. Lawrence, Tioga,
Tompkins, Warren, Washington:
Medicare
Metropolitan Life Insurance Co.
276 Genesee Street
P.O. Box 393
Utica, New York 13503

North Carolina
The Prudential Insurance Co. of America
Medicare B Division
P.O. Box 2126
High Point, North Carolina 27261

North Dakota
Medicare
Blue Shield of North Dakota
301 Eighth Street, South
Fargo, North Dakota 58102

Ohio
Medicare
Nationwide Mutual Insurance Co.
P.O. Box 57
Columbus, Ohio 43216

Oklahoma
Medicare
Aetna Life & Casualty
1140 N.W. 63rd Street
Oklahoma City, Oklahoma 73116

Oregon
Medicare
Aetna Life & Casualty
Crown Plaza
1500 S.W. First Avenue
Portland, Oregon 97201

Pennsylvania
Medicare
Pennsylvania Blue Shield
Box 65 Blue Shield Bldg.
Camp Hill, Pennsylvania 17011

Rhode Island
Medicare
Blue Shield of Rhode Island
444 Westminster Mall
Providence, Rhode Island 02901

South Carolina
Medicare
Blue Shield of South Carolina
Drawer F, Forest Acres Branch
Columbia, South Carolina 29260

South Dakota
Medicare
South Dakota Medical Services, Inc.
711 North Lake Avenue
Sioux Falls, South Dakota 57104

Tennessee
Medicare
The Equitable Life Assurance Society
P.O. Box 1465
Nashville, Tennessee 37202

Texas
Medicare
Group Medical and Surgical Service
P.O. Box 22147
Dallas, Texas 75222

Utah
Medicare
Blue Shield of Utah
P.O. Box 30270
2455 Parley's Way
Salt Lake City, Utah 84125

Vermont
Medicare
New Hampshire-Vermont
   Physician Service
Two Pillsbury Street
Concord, New Hampshire 03301

Virginia
Counties of Arlington, Fairfax;
Cities of Alexandria, Falls Church,
Fairfax:
Medicare
Medical Service of D.C.
550-12th Street., S.W.
Washington, D.C. 20024

Rest of state:
Medicare
The Travelers Insurance Co.
P.O. Box 26463
Richmond, Virginia 23261

Washington
Medicare
Washington Physicians' Service
Mail to your local Medical Service
Bureau; If you do not know which bureau
handles your claim, mail to:
Medicare Washington Physicians' Service
220 West Harrison
Seattle, Washington 98119

West Virginia
Medicare
Nationwide Mutual Insurance Co.
P.O. Box 57
Columbus, Ohio 43216

Wisconsin
County of Milwaukee:
Medicare
Surgical Care-Blue Shield
P.O. Box 2049
Milwaukee, Wisconsin 53201

Rest of state:
Medicare
Wisconsin Physicians Service
Box 1787
Madison, Wisconsin 53701

Wyoming
Medicare
The Equitable Life Assurance Society
P.O. Box 628
Cheyenne, Wyoming 82001

Puerto Rico
Medicare
Seguros De Servicio De Salud De
    Puerto Rico
P.O. Box 3628
104 Ponce de Leon Avenue
Hato Rey, Puerto Rico 00936

Virgin Islands
Medicare
Seguros De Servicio De Salud De
    Puerto Rico
P.O. Box 3628
104 Ponce de Leon Avenue
Hato Ray, Puerto Rico 00936

American Samoa
Medicare
Hawaii Medical Service Assn.
P.O. Box 860
Honolulu, Hawaii 96808

Guam
Medicare
Aetna Life & Casualty
P.O. Box 3947
Honolulu, Hawaii 96812

To handle insurance claims properly—whether governmental or private—fee setting and collecting should be standardized. Moreover, with the enactment of national health insurance, we will surely see even stricter requirements for the maintenance and presentation of patient data. For now, work toward efficiency and simplicity in record-keeping; an otherwise effective health care office is no place for a bureaucratic paperwork logjam.

CHAPTER 11

ESTATE PLANNING:
A Lifetime Job

§11.01

THE RESULTS YOU WILL GET TODAY

Do not regard estate planning as a single dismal act, reserved for the end of your life. More accurately, it involves the whole gamut of day-to-day *lifetime* decisions which may have a bearing on how secure you will leave your family.

A good estate plan performs some important *immediate* functions, like keeping your income taxes down, helping you manage your practice better, and letting you sleep at night.

Today's estate plan is a *living* plan for still another reason. The law now imposes a unified transfer tax both on lifetime gifts and on property which passes at death. Thus, today's transactions will be considered along with dispositions at death in computing your estate's tax liability—surely grist for the tax lawyer's mill.

§11.02

THERE IS MORE THAN YOUR WILL

Let's survey the territory, as we must, through the will, the bedrock of any estate plan. Around the will, all the so-called "nonprobate" assets—life insurance, living trusts, your retirement plan, powers of appointment—are built. We will touch on all of them as we guess how your lawyer might draft your will.

§11.03

THE IMPORTANCE OF DOMICILE

Its introductory clause will look something like this:

"I, Dr. Goode Planner, of Any City, Some State, make, publish, and declare this to be my will, hereby revoking any and all of my former wills and codicils."

The declaration of domicile state is important, since its laws will control the validity of the will, the place of probate, and the disposition of personal property.

§11.04

PAY "JUST DEBTS"

It is then customary to provide for the payment of "just debts." The provision is gratuitous, since Probate Acts uniformly require that all the property in an estate be subject to the payment of debts. You may want to use the clause to have your estate assume a debt thought to be questionable or one legally barred by a statute of limitations.

§11.05

THE FUNERAL EXPENSES

Next, you may want to authorize the payment of funeral expenses, incuding a suitable headstone. Setting a dollar limit will curb the zeal of overwrought relatives. All the particulars need not be detailed in your will; instructions left with your family's funeral director ought to suffice, especially since the safety deposit box where you will keep your will might not be opened until the services are over.

§11.06

GIVING YOUR BODY TO SCIENCE

You may then provide for the gift of your body or any organ, either for the use of a living person or for scientific research. The Uniform Anatomical Gift Act makes such gifts effective immediately at death and without probate.

§11.07

THE TAX IMPLICATIONS OF ESTATE PLANNING

The payment of death taxes might next be directed. A state inheritance tax may be imposed on the recipient of any gift under your will. Should you wish a gift to be received without that liability, you can have inheritance taxes paid out of the *residue* of your estate—that is, what's left after all your bequests have been fulfilled. You can do likewise with regard to federal estate taxes.

Your gross estate—the relevant assets in computing the new unified tax—will consist of these items:

(a) Property you own outright when you die.
(b) Property your spouse will receive at your death, by virtue of intestacy laws or by his or her election to take *against* your will.
(c) Gifts you make within three years of death and gifts effective at your death.
(d) All taxable gifts (those valued at more than $3,000 per recipient each year) you made since 1976.
(e) Gifts you make, withholding the right to income for life—a "life interest."
(f) Gifts you can revoke.
(g) Life insurance proceeds on your life, if you own the policy.   [See §12.02]
(h) Powers of appointment—the authority to name the beneficiary of someone else's estate.
(i) Joint tenanacies—property you own with your spouse or someone else, the survivor to take all.
(j) Lump-sum payments from qualified retirement plans.

It is significant that federal estate taxes will be levied on nonprobate assets like joint tenancy property and gifts in contemplation of death, since your state's Probate Act may require that all federal estate taxes be paid out of your estate's residue. While the Internal Revenue Code provides for the apportionment of taxes on certain nonprobate assets, it is silent as to others. To avoid penalizing your residuary beneficiary, you may want to direct that federal estate taxes be shared *pro rata* by your heirs.

§11.08

SIMULTANEOUS DEATH

You may provide for the occurrence of your death and your spouse's within a short period. Occasionally, a husband and wife will die within a few weeks of one another, as the consequence of a common disaster or of different causes. Such tragedies may result in property passing through the estate of a person who cannot enjoy it, with the attendant taxes and probate costs. There are two ways of guarding against this remote possibility:

(a) A common disaster clause:

"If my spouse and I shall die as the result of a common accident or disaster under such circumstances that it is difficult or impossible to determine which of us died first, it shall be presumed that she [he] predeceased me."

With this clause, your assets need not filter through her estate; they can go directly to your *contingent beneficiary*—your second choice to receive the property.

(b) A specified survival clause:

"I give, bequeath, and devise all the rest, residue, and remainder of my estate, real, personal, and mixed, to my wife, Mrs. Feelgood, provided that if she shall not be living on the 100th day following my death, I give, bequeath, and devise all the rest, residue, and remainder of my estate, real, personal, and mixed, to my son, Tiny Feelgood."

[See §11.10]   Note, however, that survival clauses can mean the forfeiture of the marital deduction we will talk about, so you may only want to use them if both you and your spouse have substantial estates. Otherwise, opt for the presumption that your spouse survived you.

§11.09

TAKING CARE OF YOUR SPOUSE

[See §11.07]   You will provide for your spouse's security. To start, you will want to leave your spouse the family residence—unless it is joint tenancy property which passes to the spouse automatically—the household furnishings, and any art objects and items of sentimental value. In deciding whether or not to name your spouse as residuary beneficiary, add up the income that will be received from other sources and check the effects of the "marital deduction."

§11.10

THE MARITAL DEDUCTION

A marital deduction is allowed, within narrowly defined limits, for the value of certain property, included in a decedent's estate, which passes to his or her spouse. The idea is to trade in a tax liability at the death of the first spouse, and pay the tax bill—with luck, a lower one—when the other spouse dies. Moreover, any child who is left an orphan is permitted a $5,000 deduction for each year he falls short of age 21.

The marital deduction is limited to the greater of $250,000 or 50 per cent of the *Adjusted Gross Estate*—the Gross Estate less debts and expenses. (As for gifts, either party may give the other up to $100,000 free of gift tax; a 50 per cent marital deduction applies to gifts over $200,000.)

Assume your net estate will be $400,000. Thanks to the $250,000 marital deduction, only $150,000 would be subject to tax. After applying a tax credit equivalent to a $134,000 exemption (in 1978), your total tax would be $4,800—as against $87,800 without the benefit of the marital deduction. This huge deduction can apply only to "nonterminable" interests—those that will be taxable later unless the survivor uses them up or gives them away. Here is a list of the property that qualifies:

(a) Property distributed outright under the terms of the decedent's will.
(b) Property that descends to the spouse as an intestate heir, rather than by the will.
(c) Property given as dower or in lieu of dower.
(d) Property given in contemplation of death.
(e) Property given in exercise of a power of appointment.
(f) Property held in joint tenancy, to the extent it was originally purchased with the decedent's money.
(g) Certain life insurance proceeds.
(h) Property received in an adversary will contest or in its settlement.
(i) Certain "life interests."
(j) Property passing to the spouse on account of someone else's disclaimer.

These are the rules, but how do you plan from them?

A living or testamentary trust is often the device used to make the most of the marital deduction. A marital deduction trust has at least three irresistible advantages:

(a) The estate of the first spouse to die is cut in half, and federal estate taxes are reduced accordingly.
(b) Qualifying no more than half the estate for the deduction will also reduce the estate tax the survivor's heirs will eventually pay.
(c) A trust means professional portfolio management.

A valid marital deduction trust must meet these technical requirements:

(a) The survivor must be entitled to all an interest's income, or all the income from a specific part of the interest, or a specific part of all the income—for life, payable at least annually.
(b) If the trust instrument allows income to accumulate, the survivor must have the right to demand a distribution or to receive compensation out of other assets.
(c) The survivor must be given the right to have unproductive property sold and without delay.
(d) The survivor must have an exclusive, unrestricted power to appoint the interest to herself or her estate.

Figuring exactly how much you want to qualify for the marital deduction involves some work. Sit down and make alternative assumptions about who will die first—you or your spouse—and what portion of each estate will qualify. Then add up the taxes. Remember that the deduction is the larger of $250,000 or 50 per cent of the adjusted gross estate. Table 11-1 is accurate, but not really complete. For one thing, a credit against the "tentative tax" shown has been written into the law. It varies by year—$34,000 in 1978, $38,000 in 1979, $42,500 in 1980, and $47,000 in 1981 and thereafter. For another, most estates are entitled to other credits not taken into account here, including a credit for state death taxes paid.

Table 11–1 UNIFIED GIFT AND ESTATE TAX RATES

IF TAXABLE AMOUNT IS—		THE TAX IS—		
Over	But not over	This-	Plus %	Over
$ 0	$ 10,000	$ 0	18	$ 0
10,000	20,000	1,800	20	10,000
20,000	40,000	3,800	22	20,000
40,000	60,000	8,200	24	40,000
60,000	80,000	13,000	26	60,000
80,000	100,000	18,200	28	80,000
100,000	150,000	23,800	30	100,000
150,000	250,000	38,800	32	150,000
250,000	500,000	70,800	34	250,000
500,000	750,000	155,800	37	500,000
750,000	1,000,000	248,300	39	750,000
1,000,000	1,250,000	345,800	41	1,000,000
1,250,000	1,500,000	448,300	43	1,250,000
1,500,000	2,000,000	555,800	45	1,500,000
2,000,000	2,500,000	780,800	49	2,000,000
2,500,000	3,000,000	1,025,800	53	2,500,000
3,000,000	3,500,000	1,290,800	57	3,000,000
3,500,000	4,000,000	1,575,800	61	3,500,000
4,000,000	4,500,000	1,880,800	65	4,000,000
4,500,000	5,000,000	2,205,800	69	4,500,000
5,000,000		2,550,800	70	5,000,000

§11.11

ALL YOUR BEQUESTS

You may choose to make some other bequests. The odds are you will have all kinds of personal property to give under your will's terms. To the extent you can do it by bequest, the recipients will not have any income tax to pay on receipt; as residuary beneficiaries receiving proceeds after a sale, they might.

Basically, there are three kinds of bequests:

(a) *Specific* bequests. We are talking about giving one special chattel, like leaving Johnny the '78 T-Bird.
(b) *General* bequests. We're talking about a gift that can be satisfied out of the estate's general assets, like leaving $1,000 to Jimmy.

(c) *Demonstrative* bequests. We're talking about a money gift to be paid from a designated source, like leaving $500 to Susie, payable out of your account at the First National.

What if you make some bequests of each kind, but the assets just are not sufficient to fulfill your gifts? They are said to *abate*—that is, to be diminished. Unless you specify otherwise, the residuary estate will abate first, then the general bequests, and the specific bequests last.

Suppose you will Johnny the T-Bird in 1978, but sell it in 1979. The bequest will be subject to *ademption* and be voided. Demonstrative bequests represent an exception to the rule. If monies are bequeathed out of a fund which no longer exists, the gift can be satisfied out of the general assets of the estate.

One caveat: all cash bequests are payable before other categories of beneficiaries receive anything. You may want to provide that certain cash bequests are to be paid only if the estate exceeds a specified size.

§11.12

REMEMBER CHARITY

Make your charitable bequests. Both personal satisfaction and tax benefits inure to the testator who makes a gift to his church or a charitable organization. Safeguard your gift by formally identifying the intended recipient; its address would be helpful to mention. Make sure the institution is well-established and likely to survive you, so your gift won't be defeated. And don't unduly restrict the use of your gift; the limitations you impose might frustrate the charity's preconceived planning.

As for tax incentives, bequests to exempt charities are excluded from a decedent's taxable estate. To be sure if this advantage applies to your favorite charity, write the Superintendent of Documents, U.S. Government Printing Office, Washington, D.C., for the current "Cumulative List of Organizations described in Section 17(C) of the Internal Revenue Code of 1954."

§11.13

WHAT ABOUT LAND?

Devises will come next. These are gifts of interest in real estate. The crucial thing here is to understand what you are giving. First, your spouse may have unavoidable *dower* or *curtesy* rights. What's more, your gift of land may well include a "gift" of the mortgage debt that encumbers it, even if your loan is executed after the will is signed. If you do not intend that result, your will should say so. This is a telling example of how today's business decision can affect the provisions of yesterday's will. Clearly, estate planning must be a continuous activity, not an hour in your lawyer's office.

§11.14

SAFEGUARDING YOUR CHILDREN'S FUTURE

You may want to appoint a guardian for minor children. That is important even if both parents are now alive, since there is no guarantee either will live until all minors reach adulthood. The designation of a guardian will not deprive a surviving parent of the right of child custody. Typically, two guardians are appointed: a close relative as guardian of the person and a trust company as guardian of the estate.

§11.15

CLASS GIFTS

You may provide for a *class* gift. If you want all your nephews or grandchildren to share a sum of money—regardless of how many of these beneficiaries there may be at your death—you intend a class gift. Precise language is mandatory when it comes to (a) defining the class, and (b) prescribing how they are to share.

§11.16

HOW TO USE A TRUST

[See §4.06]   Whenever a greater duty is to be imposed on an administrator of estate assets than an executor would commonly have, create a testamentary trust. You can spell out all kinds of special requirements, while not impeding the estate's probate. Trusts are often used when a charity is a beneficiary and customarily when a child is to be an heir. A trust can sidestep the appointment of a guardian, who would be forced to post a bond and furnish the court with costly periodic accountings.

In many states, property can be "poured over" from your estate to a living trust—one that can take advantage of the marital deduction and some death tax savings. Consider the on-going estate planning possibilities.

§11.17

WHO GETS EVERYTHING ELSE?

The final dispositive clause will be the residuary clause. Give serious consideration to other property-transferring devices you are using—insurance, living trusts, joint tenancies, lifetime gifts—when you decide who is going to get everything you have not otherwise bequeathed. Nonprobate benefits and the marital deduction trust will probably have left your spouse well cared for, so there is a good chance you will want to pay the residue to a testamentary trust, with your children as beneficiaries.

§11.18

NAMING AN EXECUTOR

You will want to name an executor to manage your estate and carry out your instructions. Look for skill and experience. You can waive the customary bond, if you wish.

§11.19

THE WITNESSES

Sign your will and have it properly witnessed by three witnesses, even if local law requires only two. The will's "prove-up," years later, may be an easier job.

§11.20

PLANNING IS THE ANSWER

Your will is the basic element in a continuing estate planning program, geared to both present and future goals. When your will, your insurance package, your living trusts and gifts, your joint tenancies and powers of appointment, and your retirement program are integrated as a unit—only then will you be assured of effectively achieving your objectives.

CHAPTER **12**

INSURANCE:
The Great
Risk Controller

§12.01

PLAYING IT SAFE

Whenever you visit your lawyer's office, most of your questions probably boil down to this one: "how can I best protect myself?" You may be thinking about minimizing risks, reducing tax liabilities, or planning for the future, but self-protection, in its broadest meaning, is the goal.

In this book, we have suggested many ways attorneys can help health professionals make the most of opportunities and avoid pitfalls—to protect themselves in general. Insurance, not arbitrarily, has been saved for last: your insurance contracts represent the pinnacle of legal self-protection.

We live at a time when every act from birth to death has legal consequences. Some are unpredictable and uncontrollable; others we can try to guard against and hope for the best. With insurance—and sometimes only with insurance—we are promised that a given result will indeed happen. We are buying definable legal and psychological protection. We are confining our risks to preordained limits with a steel-trap certainty to be found almost nowhere else. If legal planning strives to guarantee positive results and to avoid surprise adversities, insurance stands out as its most effective tool.

It is fitting that insurance be reserved as the last topic we discuss for another reason. The variation and complexity one finds in insurance contracts require a sweeping appreciation for many branches of the law, an appreciation it is hoped you have gained in reading this handbook thus far.

§12.02

THE BOUNTIES OF LIFE INSURANCE

No form of coverage has as many faces or as many personalities as life insurance. Look at all it can do for you, your family, and your practice:

[See §11.07]
1. Obviously, life insurance can pay the costs that death brings with it—estate taxes and all the rest.

2. Life insurance can pay off a policyholder's mortgage in the event of death before payment completion.
3. Life insurance policies, especially "endowment policies," are often used to finance college costs. While you cannot expect the high rate of return many securities offer, life insurance can pay your children's way through school.
4. If you are a corporate employee, life insurance can fund any deferred compensation vehicle—and that includes your retirement plan. [See Chapter 4]
5. Life insurance can fund a corporate stock redemption or cross-purchase agreement. [See §3.03]
6. Life insurance can fund a partnership's buy-sell agreement. [See §1.05]
7. Finally, life insurance can protect a practice from the extraordinary expense associated with losing a "key person"—yourself or your colleague.

§12.03

HOW TO JUDGE YOUR LIFE POLICY

It is beyond challenge that you need life insurance for some of these reasons and perhaps for others not mentioned. Exactly which policy, though? Costs, benefits, dividends, and cash value vary so much that comparing one policy with another is awfully frustrating.

The "net cost" method was once the accepted way of judging what a policy really gives you for your dollar. "Net cost" means the average surrendered net cost per $1,000 of coverage. Here is how it is figured:

TAKE the total premiums the policyholder pays over a period of years.
SUBTRACT the dividends the company pays out.
SUBTRACT any cash value.
DIVIDE by the number of years.
AND YOU HAVE FOUND the yearly cost of insurance.
DIVIDE that amount by the number of thousands of dollars of coverage.
AND YOU HAVE COMPUTED the insurance cost per year per $1,000 of insurance coverage.

The "net cost" method is helpful in evaluating life policies. Another method does the job even better. The Joint Special Committee on Life Insurance Costs, representing most of the important life insurers, advocates the "interest-adjusted" method for comparing policies.

The "interest-adjusted" method questions how these premium dollars would fare if the prospective policyholder put them in a savings bank instead of buying insurance with them. Sure, that inquiry is not as comprehensive as it ought to be, and it has some built-in flaws:

- First, it looks at costs narrowly. You might be happy to pay a little more and gain a policy feature or two.
- It assumes that you are surrendering your policy for its cash value. Maybe you never will.
- Dividends are projected, and the person who estimates them might be greatly in error.

As a quick and easy barometer for measuring one life policy against another, though, the "interest-adjusted" method has several advantages over the "net cost" method:

- For one thing, "interest-adjusted" analysis takes a harder look at the costs you are to pay. You will not only be paying premiums; you will also be losing the investment income these dollars could have earned elsewhere. Thus, the "cost-adjusted" method does not just add up your premiums; it *accumulates* them at 4 per cent a year after taxes.
- This method does the same with dividends.
- For the same reason, dividing accumulated premiums less accumulated dividends and cash value by the number of years to arrive at the annual cost of insurance is shortsighted. The "interest-adjusted" method would have you divide your result by a factor that takes lost interest into account.

We said that the "interest-adjusted" method compares the cost of your life insurance protection with the protection a bank account might give you. What is its big advantage over the "net cost" approach? Accuracy. Consider an example taken from the Joint Special Committee's Report:

Age	35
Coverage	$10,000
Annual premium	240
Annual dividend	18, increasing by $6 each year
Cash value, starting the second year, increasing by $190 each year.	

The net cost analysis looks like this:

Total premiums over 20 years	$ 4,800.00
LESS: Total dividends	–1,500.00
LESS: Cash value	–3,610.00
Insurance cost	–$ 310.00

That is –$15.50 per year or –$1.55 per thousand dollars of insurance coverage—cheaper than free! Something is obviously missing, and it's a lost interest factor. See how the "interest-adjusted" method brings the evaluation within reason:

Premiums accumulated at interest over 20 years	$ 7,433.00
LESS: Dividends accumulated at interest	–2,003.00
LESS: Cash value	–3,610.00
The difference	$ 1,820.00
DIVIDED BY: the 20-year factor, $30,969	$ 0.0588

That is $5.88 per year for each $1,000 worth of insurance protection, a believable rate. The analysis is a worthwhile one, but note a few shortcomings:

- The "interest-adjusted" method contrasts policies at the time benefits are paid, not when the policies are purchased.

- Forget about the "interest-adjusted" method if you are looking at a term policy—those that are scheduled to expire automatically on a given date; they do not have much, if any, cash value.
- Do not use the method to compare a policy you own now with one you might want to buy. The new one has to cost more. In addition, cash values plod upward at a snail's pace; the cash value your present policy has built up will not be matched by a new policy for a long time.
- The "interest-adjusted" approach is not very helpful in comparing interest-paying with noninterest-paying policies, either.

What we have suggested is a fair way of judging values in "ordinary," permanent life insurance, the granddaddy of all the imaginative policy forms your insurance broker has told you about. Whole life, as it is sometimes called, has a level premium cost—more than adequate to provide the agreed insurance protection during the early years of coverage, but less than adequate later on. The insurance company's secret is investing in bonds and mortgages. The excess premium dollars you pay in the first few years grow into cash reserves, capable of paying claims years later. The principle is pretty straightforward.

§12.04

A NEW BREED OF LIFE POLICIES

There is a good chance, however, that you may need a special policy, one that has a feature or two out of the "ordinary." Here are a few other life policies worth pondering:

1. *Term life.* Suppose you do not think your total insurance needs at retirement will be as great as they are now. You will have substantial savings and a profitable investment portfolio; your children will be on their own, and you will have less responsibility. So why insure your life into your 70s and beyond? Maybe you should not. Term insurance protects you for a given period of time only. It is the least expensive kind of life insurance. True, it does not build up much cash value; and, of course, premiums go up as you get older, but you may find that perfectly acceptable.

2. *Split life.* This is a combination term life policy and an annuity, calling for the company's payment to the purchaser of a fixed amount in installments. You would pay a level premium for the annuity, an increasing annual premium for the term insurance—and the two benefits can be split between two people. With an annuity, the term insurance might sell for about half its usual cost.

   Note this special situation in which split life funding looks right: young Doctor A wants to buy out old Doctor B for $100,000, payable over ten years. Doctor B takes the cash payments and buys term life coverage on Doctor A's life. It is cheap; Doctor A is young. If Doctor A dies before the installment contract is fulfilled, the practice is paid for anyway.

3. *Adjustable life.* This "life cycle" coverage combines term and whole life. Premiums can be cut by reducing the term of coverage or by switching from whole life to term as your financial facts of life change.

4. *Variable life.* What the life insurance policyholder has always regretted is his purchase's inability to cope with runaway inflation. About 60 insurance companies have now sold a product to about a million customers who think they've licked the problem.

   Variable life is part insurance, part investment. Purchasers pay a set premium. Their death benefits are geared to the performance of a reserve fund consisting of pooled premiums invested in the stock market. As inflation trims the dollar's purchasing power, a rise in stock prices should create more and more dollars in death benefits.

Even if all does not work out as planned, every policyholder will be assured of a minimum death benefit, guaranteed at policy purchase time. These are the minimum proceeds payable at death:

If the policy is bought at age . . .	The minimum death benefit for every $100 of annual premium is . . .
35	$3,300
40	$2,700
45	$2,100
50	$1,500
55	$1,300

Variable life policies are subject to the "full disclosure" requirements of the Securities and Exchange Commission and to the insurance laws of your state. Explore the variable route.

§12.05

THE FORM OF YOUR LIFE INSURANCE PURCHASE

Once you have decided on your policy, structure your purchase. There are a number of attractive ways to consider buying life coverage:

[See §4.06]

1. Put your policy in a trust. That way, beneficiaries will save some money and make some money. A lifetime trust—one set up today instead of being part of your will— can avoid probate with its various fees and executor's commissions, up to 10 per cent of your policy's value. You will reduce inheritance taxes and save from 2 to 15 per cent, depending on the state you live in. What's more, you can instruct the trustee to invest dividends in any category of investment you like; your beneficiaries will have gained a pretty good hedge against inflation, especially if proceeds are made payable in installments.

There are two kinds of trusts, *revocable* and *irrevocable*. A revocable trust lets you change beneficiaries, amend the payout method, or even revoke the trust altogether. You'll keep all that authority, and as we have seen, your beneficiaries will still gain.

An irrevocable trust requires that you give your policies away and relinquish your rights. For that sacrifice, you'll get a bonus: a big federal estate tax saving, probably around 10 per cent of your policy's face value. There are two drawbacks:

[See §12.07]

(a) Your spouse will lose the $1,000 interest exemption we'll talk about.
(b) Trusts cost money to operate.

It is recommended that you consider an insurance trust only when proceeds will be substantial.

2. Give your policy away as soon as you buy it. The idea is a natural correlate to the irrevocable trust idea. When you assign your policy absolutely, only a small gift tax may be payable, the gift's value being established by reference to comparable policies sold by the insurer. The ultimate proceeds will completely escape federal estate taxes.

One caveat: any gift given within three years of the donor's death will be taxed as part of the estate.

3. Have your spouse buy a policy on your life. All you will have to do is submit yourself for a physical, and your spouse will do the rest, even make all the premium payments. As the absolute owners of policies, spouses have the unrestricted ability to name beneficiaries; they can, in fact, name themselves. Your spouse will want to name your child as contingent owner of the policy, and leave its cash value to the child in a will, so the policy cannot possibly revert to your estate if your spouse dies before you do.

Your spouse can borrow against the policy and exercise every other right, too. There will be no gift tax to pay and no probate costs, either. Moreover, if your spouse wishes, part of the proceeds can be loaned to your executor to pay your estate's taxes or debts. A word of warning: your spouse cannot be forced to loan policy proceeds; if any strings are attached to a spouse's free ownership, all the proceeds are includible in your taxable estate.

§12.06

A WIFE'S LIFE COVERAGE

If you are a male health professional, we know that your life insurance decisions are intertwined with your wife's future. That is not very surprising. What about the coin's other side? Should you buy coverage on your wife's life?

Your wife is irreplacable. That is obvious. Life insurance will not ease the emotional pain were you to lose her, however. So reduce the inquiry to objective terms and look only at the dollars involved. Were your wife to die before you, you would incur at least some of these expenses:

1. Her medical and hospital bills.
2. Funeral expenses.
3. Domestic help, including a nursemaid for the children.
4. More estate tax for your survivors. Without a surviving wife, there would be no marital deduction.

Your wife's death would mean more outgo and less cash income—the lost income from her employment as well as the Social Security benefits payable to her from her 62nd birthday.

With all these arguments, good life insurance salesmen have an easy job before them when they try to sell a professional man a policy on his wife's life. You probably ought to resist the temptation to buy.

Your prime concern should be adequate coverage for yourself—at least five or six times your annual income. If you are the principal breadwinner, it is your death that would spell financial disaster. If you are the source of the bulk of your family's income, you can cost-justify big insurance premiums on your own life, but, unless she makes a very significant financial contribution to the family, not on your wife's. Be cautious, but not extreme: add a rider to your own policy, insuring your wife's life for $10,000 or less. That amount will cover the initial financial burden should she die before you. You may want to consider buying a family plan package policy. It is inexpensive and will cover your wife and your children until they reach the age of 21, at which time they would have the right to convert their policies to longer lasting ones.

§12.07

LIFE INSURANCE AND THE TAX LAWS

Now let's talk taxes. Tax consequences will always be in the forefront of a life insurance decision, and life insurance is beautifully tax-privileged:

- Any life insurance beneficiary receives lump-sum death proceeds income tax-free.
- A beneficiary who receives installment payments pays income tax only on that part of a payment which represents interest earned after the death of a policyholder.
- The widow gets a special tax break. If she gets principal-and-interest installments, the principal she gets is tax-free, just as it would be for any other beneficiary. Interest is tax-free too—up to $1,000 a year. Be careful, though: income of proceeds left with the insurance company under an "interest option" is not tax-free, and the tax exemption is lost if the proceeds are put in trust.

[See §11.10]
- If the policyholder owns the policy at his or her death, proceeds are federal estate-taxable, of course. They can qualify for the marital deduction, however, which keeps taxes way down.

§12.08

HOW TO TAKE THE BENEFITS

Note also the tax effect of these "settlement options"—typical ways in which proceeds are payable:

1. A beneficiary can leave the proceeds with the insurance company and earn interest. Interest, as always, is ordinary taxable income.
2. A beneficiary can receive payments for a period of years in an amount which, with interest, will exhaust the proceeds. Each payment is taxable except that part which is deemed a return of capital.
3. A beneficiary can get income periodically until proceeds plus interest are used up. One will gain from a periodic payout program.
4. Guaranteed life annuities are fairly common. Periodic payments are made to policyholders as long as they live. If they die before receiving an agreed number of payments, the beneficiary gets the balance. The tax analysis is tricky: multiply the annual payouts by the policyholder's life expectancy to compute the expected return. Compare total premiums paid to the expected return and determine what fraction of the expected return is the premium investment. That fraction of every year's income is tax-free, even if the policyholder lives beyond his or her life expectancy.

§12.09

PROFESSIONAL LIABILITY COVERAGE

[See Chapter 8]
While life insurance is the most versatile, multifunctional form of protection, malpractice coverage is the most basic to the continuing performance of your professional duties. Without it, your financial exposure is boundless, and virtually any treatment you undertake to perform is carried out at a grave personal risk.

No malpractice policy is perfect, and all of them are unintelligible to a nonlawyer. Since premium fluctuation is minimal, you will want to buy the most comprehensive policy you can; have your lawyer confirm that that is what you are getting.

It may be a good idea to obtain your premises liability and malpractice coverage from the same insurer, so you will not be caught in the middle of a dispute over which policy applies. If you are a partner, buy your policy where your co-partners buy theirs; if you are a corporate employee, buy your individual policy where the corporation buys its; the defense of a joint lawsuit will be tremendously simplified.

How much should you buy? At the very least $100,000 per individual, $300,000 per occurrence. In addition, buy a $1,000,000 umbrella policy. It will supplement your professional liability, personal liability, and other coverage; it is a truly wise investment. Shop around, consult your professional association for leads, and make your dollar outlay cost-effective.

What should the policy cover? The best of policies will protect you in these ways:

- You are protected against any claim or lawsuit which arises from services you rendered or should have rendered. That means negligence or breach of contract.
- You are protected against claims arising out of the performance of your duties as a member of a professional group. Here we mean defamation of character.
- You are defended even against a fraudulent claim.
- You are assured the company will not settle without your consent. You might not want a compromise when your reputation is at stake.
- Your employees are covered. Remember, you may be responsible for their acts.
- Your protection is not diminished by the fact that you may own other policies.

§12.10

OTHER POLICIES FOR YOUR PRACTICE

Your malpractice insurance is only one kind of protection you need at the office. Here are some others worth mentioning:

1. *Fire.* This is a necessity if you own your office building or if your lease gives you the fire insurance obligation.

   Insurance companies usually require that the owner act as a co-insurer. If the owner does not insure the property to a prescribed minimum, often 80 per cent, he or she will be underinsured, even if a loss is only partial. Your failure to co-insure adequately will reduce the insurance company's obligation. Suppose your building's insurable value is $100,000, and your policy requires 80 per cent co-insurance. If you carry only $40,000 in insurance coverage, you have complied only halfway. If your building has a $10,000 fire loss, the company is obliged to pay out only halfway and give you $5,000.

   Protect yourself. Do 5 per cent better than the clause requires. The premium increment will be negligible, and you will leave room for error and appreciation.

2. *Owners', Landlords', and Tenants' Liability (OL & T).* OL & T insures against claims which might result from your lease or ownership of a building—or even your operation of it. It will spell out all the risks it covers. Safe policy limits are $100,000 per person/$300,000 per occurrence.

3. *Multiperil.* This is a package policy typically insuring against fire, burglary and theft, office contents, professional equipment, and general liability. It is a godsend at coping with overlapping and gapping coverage dilemmas, and genuinely a terrific idea.

§12.11

THE COVERAGE EVERYONE NEEDS

At home, you have about the same insurance needs everyone else does:

1. *Homeowners.* Protect your investment against fire, lighting, and the like. If your house is mortgaged, the mortgage lender will want your policy limits high enough to cover the mortgage debt even if your house is destroyed. Premiums run about $2 per $1,000 of coverage—more with "extended coverage" against hail and windstorm, explosion, riot, even falling trees or crashing cars. Buy coverage with a $500 deductible and you will save about 25 per cent.

2. *Personal property.* Your valuables are covered at home and away for about $2.50 per $1,000 coverage. To validate your coverage, keep receipts for all major purchases or, if unavailable, take photos of items as they can be seen in your house. Maintain an inventory, too. You will be able to prove you once had what you are claiming is now gone.

    If there is a theft, be sure to call the police immediately, or you may have a difficult time collecting from the insurance company.

3. *Personal liability.* Protect yourself against legal liability in the nonvehicular accidents in which you could find yourself involved. The cost is $1 per $1,000 coverage and up.

[See §3.01]

4. *Hospitalization.* If you are a corporate employee, you know you can contract to have the corporation pay the costs and deduct them.

5. *Disability.* Again, a corporation can deduct the premiums it pays for its employees.

6. *Automobile.* Auto policies in most states have five kinds of coverage:

    (a) Liability. This is a must. You are protected if you cause an accident which results in personal injury, property damage, or both. The insurance company will defend you in court and pay all claims against you up to the policy limits: from $10,000 to $100,000 for one person injured or killed; from $20,000 to $300,000 for more than one person injured or killed in the same accident; plus $5,000 or more for property damage.

    Many states require liability. Even if yours does not, buy an adequate amount. Avoid having to put your life savings on the line.

    (b) Collision. The insurance company will pay for damage done to your car less a deductible—usually between $100 and $500—even if you were at fault. The coverage may be unnecessary if your car is not fairly new; its value—less the deductible—is the maximum recovery.

    If you buy a collision policy, opt for a big deductible. A $300 deductible does not substantially increase your risk over a $100 deductible, but it does lower your premium dramatically.

    (c) Comprehensive. Protect yourself against just about everything but a collision—fire, theft, you name it. Comprehensive auto insurance is inexpensive and valuable coverage. Elect deductible coverage, not "actual cash value"; you'll save in premiums.

    (d) Medical payments. These cover the expenses you and your passengers might incur if injured—even the ambulance bill—no matter who is responsible for an accident. The limit is usually no lower than $500, no higher than $5,000.

    (e) Uninsured motorists. The coverage defines itself. It protects you against personal injuries caused by an uninsured driver. Many states require UM, and they are wise to do so.

Auto insurance nationwide is on the verge of an overhaul, and with ample justification. Premiums are frighteningly high; courts are clogged with tiny nuisance claims; and huge "pain and suffering" settlements are slow and often inequitable.

By way of a solution, proposals for one or another "no-fault" auto insurance plan are making their way through most state legislatures. Most will be tabled or sent to committees and reworked, but eventually no fault insurance will be law. Payments for wages lost and out-of-pocket expenses will be made promptly to the passengers of insured vehicles without regard to who may have caused an accident. Except in extreme cases, damages for pain and suffering will be limited by statute. The result will be lower insurance costs for everyone. Watch no-fault happen and applaud.

§12.12
A RESPONSIBLE LEGAL SYSTEM

The advent of no-fault auto insurance is typical of insurance law and indeed of law in general. As risks exceed reasonable expectations, society steps in and recreates the balance, for fairness and for progress. This is the strength of our legal system which, with due regard and due respect, can be relied upon to help each of us grow.

INDEX